The House of Treason

Theory or Reality

Ronald L. Waldron

authorHOUSE®

AuthorHouse™
1663 Liberty Drive
Bloomington, IN 47403
www.authorhouse.com
Phone: 1-800-839-8640

First published by AuthorHouse   7/8/2009

ISBN: 978-1-4490-0537-5 (sc)

Printed in the United States of America
Bloomington, Indiana

This book is printed on acid-free paper.

God, Jesus and Allah do not ask for belief behind the barrel of a gun!

In GOD we trust, or any reference to GOD is belief by all religions. It does not single out Christian. It does not say "Jesus Christ". It seems to include Jews, Muslims, and Native
American spirituality, or any other belief.

That is separation from any one religion.

"It's true you can't judge a book by its cover, but you can tell a lot about a person by what he or she reads."
The facts show that naive (deficient in worldly wisdom or informed judgment) America does not read. They are not informed or care to be. That has led us to the place we find ourselves in. catastrophic failures and corruption.

Corrupt Israeli PM - has a stake in a corrupt Israeli bank- owned by a corrupt Wall Street global hedge fund - which owns a corrupt US defense contractor - which contributes to corrupt GOP Congressmen - who also receive money from another corrupt defense contractor - that defense contractor produced faulty intel under contract to a corrupt CIA Assn't Director - that faulty intel was used to justify a corrupt US Administration's case for invading Iraq - that was planned and executed by corrupt neocons inside DoD who had written a proposal years earlier to wage wars to privatize the Israeli economy.

What a tangled web. One wishes Chairman Waxman's staff and other Congressional investigators the strength of Hercules in taking down the Three-headed Dog, Cerberus, that guards the gates to Hell.

What becomes of public space, or the commons, when everything is privatized? It is not only our tax monies, but our freedoms, that are being stolen.

A large global hedge fund, Cerberus Capital Management (dba, Cerberus-Gabriel), is at the center of an emerging Pentagon and CIA contracting scandal

In each case, the companies under investigation have links to prominent GOP figures, including former Vice President Dick Cheney, former Vice President Dan Quayle, former Defense Secretary Donald Rumsfeld, and several Republican Congressmen indicted for corruption involving kickbacks from defense contractors. The National Republican Congressional Committee (NRCC) has also received substantial contributions from conservative fund managers running Cerberus, a virtually unregulated $30 billion hedge fund, which owns the second largest bank in Israel.

This scandal involves the mismanagement of VA hospital facilities privatized during the Bush-Cheney Administration, as well as intelligence abuses by private CIA contractors.
Cerberus owns, or had a major interest in, a string of now-bankrupt companies that had contracts with U.S. defense and intelligence agencies that were found to have a common pattern of large-scale fraud, security problems, and financial scandals involving GOP lawmakers and lobbyists.

Now we are experiencing the same foreign and corporate lobbies buying up both sides of the Isle, The corruption has spread further, because we the people allow it, we seem to expect it and simply ignore it. Will we ever stop being mindless?

Now it seems the torture issues are being influenced not to release the involvement of Mossad & Blackwater in the training and carrying out the torture referred to. Keep it to blaming the little guy. Our troops, those are at the bottom of the accountability list.

Just months before the invasion, DoD designated Halliburton/KBR as the sole potential bidder for potential large-scale pipeline repair contracts. Four years after the initial invasion and occupation of those fields, Iraq is still not producing at its prewar levels, a threshold that would require termination of the RIO contract.

The fundraisers, which take place and the subsequent vote, illustrate the kind of relationship between congressman and contributor that's under increased scrutiny in the nation's capital.

Steve Rosen, Accused Aipac Spy, Joins Jewish Anti-Obama Media:

This is for all of you out there who sincerely believe that Aipac is a non-partisan, fair-minded, centrist group. You'll recall the story of Steve Rosen (at the time Aipac's chief political operative) and Keith Weissman, allegedly caught red-handed by the FBI accepting secret U.S. government documents from Pentagon analyst Larry Franklin. The pre-trial motions have dragged on for a few years.

The indicted Rosen is basically unemployable by any of the pro-Israel political groups, think tanks, PACs or politicians that might hire him. Apparently tired of stewing in his own juices, he's affiliated with several far-right Jewish media enterprises. He's begun, Obama Mideast Monitor, whose home is at Daniel Pipes' Middle East Forum. The blog promises to probe Obama's Israel policy and foreign policy appointments with a fine tooth comb looking for 'anti-Israel' tendencies. He's also become a contributor to American Thinker, ** home of some of the farthest right anti-Obama smear mongering during the last campaign. All that remains is for Rosen to publish in American Thinker's sister publication (ideologically), FrontPage magazine. That'll come I guess. Rosen has made his hard-right political bed and now he's happy to lie in it.But Steve is attempting to take the high road and gamely denying any partisan intent:

"One should not assume that the purpose of this blog is to draw a negative picture of a future Obama administration's views toward the Middle East," Rosen told the Forward, adding that he does not necessarily agree with all the views of the Middle East Forum, which is hosting his blog. I'd like to ask him which specific militantly pro-Israel, anti-Obama, and anti-Arab views of Daniel Pipes does the former "not necessarily agree with?" Or was Rosen so desperate to "get back in the game" that he took the only offer he could get, from the likes of Pipes.

While I'm not an attorney, I find it astonishing that someone indicted for allegedly passing state secrets to Israel would hitch their wagon to such militantly pro-Israel enterprises. Doesn't he thereby reinforce the notion that his original commitment in accepting the documents was to aid Israel's intelligence capabilities? And doesn't that in turn help the government prosecution in making its case against him? Besides, isn't throwing in your lot with two harshly anti-Obama Jewish sites basically sticking your finger in the eye of the new president and daring him to redouble the government's efforts to win a conviction?

I also find it rather astonishing that he's writing specifically about Bush Administration policy toward Iran, precisely the subject that brought him to the FBI's attention in the first place. His motivation, from what I can tell, appears at least partially to embarrass Bush, who he must blame for his legal troubles. Additionally, his goal seems to be to point out the perfidy and evil represented by the Iranian regime. It may raise his polemical hackles should an Obama Administration go all soft inside and stoop to negotiating with the Ayatollahs. All this has me scratching my head saying: "Huh?" Does this guy know what he's doing?

Rosen has high-priced and high-profile Washington legal representation in Abbe Lowell. So I find it hard to believe that his attorney would tell him to plow ahead with these projects. But I guess I'm wrong. What do I know? But then again, I'm not on trial for espionage and Rosen is.

Rosen's current affiliations also go a long way toward explaining what his views were when he worked for 23 years for the 'non-partisan, centrist' Aipac. So much for the truth of that claim. Aipac, like Rosen, has always interpreted pro-Israel as being pro-nationalist and pro-Likud. They were birds of a feather.

The Obama Administration needs to signal that the US is preparing to remove the training wheels from Israel's "free ride" enabled by American tax-payers?
BUT is he caving in to their machine.

Calm Voice, Big Stick:

BARACK OBAMA is often compared to Franklin Delano Roosevelt, but it is from the book of another Roosevelt that he has taken a leaf: President Theodore Roosevelt, who, 108 years ago, advised his successors: "Speak softly and carry a big stick!"

This week, the whole world saw how this is done. Obama sat in the Oval Office side by side with Binyamin Netanyahu and spoke to the journalists. He was earnest, but relaxed. The body language spoke clearly: while Netanyahu leaned forward assiduously, like a traveling salesman peddling his merchandise, Obama leaned back, tranquil and self-assured. He spoke softly, very softly. But leaning against the wall behind him, hidden by the flag, was a very big stick indeed. THE WORLD wanted, of course, to know what went on between the two when they met alone.

Coming home, Netanyahu strenuously tried to present the meeting as a great success. But after the spotlights turned off and the red carpet rolled up, we can examine what we have really seen and heard. Among his great achievements, Netanyahu emphasized the Iranian issue. "We have reached complete agreement," he proudly announced time and again.

Wait a minute. What is that we hear, "military"? Where did this word creep up from? Until now, all Israeli governments have insisted that Iran must be prevented from acquiring any nuclear capability at all. The new formula means that the Netanyahu government now accepts Iran having a "non-military"– which is never very far from a "military" - nuclear capability.

This is not Netanyahu's only defeat on the Iranian issue. Before his trip, he demanded that Obama give Iran just three months, "until October", and that after this "all the options would be on the table". An ultimatum, that included a military threat.

Obama said that he would conduct a dialogue with Iran until the end of the year, and that he would then assess what had been achieved and consider what to do next. If he came to the conclusion that there had been no progress, he would take further steps, including the imposition of more stringent sanctions. The military option has disappeared. True, before the meeting Obama told a newspaper that "all the options are on the table", but the fact that he did not repeat this in Netanyahu's presence speaks volumes.

No doubt Netanyahu asked for permission to attack Iran, or – at the very least – to threaten such an attack. The answer was a flat No. Obama is resolved to prevent an Israeli attack. He has warned the Israeli government unequivocally. Just to make sure that the message has been properly absorbed, he sent the CIA chief to Israel to deliver the message personally to every Israeli leader.

The Israeli plan for a military attack on Iran has been taken off the table – if it was ever lying there.

Netanyahu wanted to connect Iran with the Palestinian issue, in a negative way: as long as the Iranian danger exists, the Palestinian matter cannot be dealt with. Obama has turned the formula upside down and made a positive connection: progress on the Palestinian issue is a precondition to progress on the Iranian one. That makes sense: the unsolved conflict is fuelling Iran, provides it with a reason to menace Israel and weakens the opposition of Egypt and Saudi Arabia to Iran's ambitions.

OBAMA'S MAIN message concerned one issue that returned to center stage this week: Settlements. This word almost disappeared during the reign of Bush the Younger. True, all US administrations have opposed the enlargement of the settlements, but since the failed attempt by James Baker, the Secretary of State of Bush the Elder, to impose sanctions on Israel, no one has dared to do anything about them. In Washington they mumbled, on the ground they built. In Jerusalem they dissimulated, and on the ground they built. "We are negotiating about dividing the pizza; in the meantime, Israel is eating it."

It has to be repeated again and again: the settlements are a disaster for the Palestinians, a disaster for peace and a double and triple disaster for Israel. First, because their main aim is to make the establishment of a Palestinian state impossible, and thus prevent peace forever. Second, because they suck the marrow out of the Israeli economy and swallow resources that should be used to help the poor. Third: because the settlements undermine the rule of law in Israel, they spread the cancer of fascism and push the whole political system to the right.

Obama is right when he puts the settlement issue ahead of everything else, even ahead of the peace negotiations. A total cessation of building in the settlements comes before anything else. When a body is bleeding, the flow has to be stopped before the disease can be treated. Otherwise the patient will die of loss of blood and there won't be anybody left to treat. This is precisely the aim of Netanyahu.

This is why Netanyahu has refused to accede to the request. Otherwise his coalition would have fallen apart and he would be compelled to resign or set up an alternative coalition with Kadima. The hapless Tzipi Livni, who has not found a role in opposition, would probably jump at the opportunity.

Netanyahu will try to use Barak against Barack. With the help of Ehud Barak he is putting on a performance of "demolishing outposts", in order to divert attention from the ongoing building in the settlements. We shall see whether this ploy succeeds and whether the settlers' leadership will play their part in this charade. The day after Netanyahu's return, Barak demolished for the seventh time (!) Maoz Esther, an outpost consisting of seven wooden huts. Within hours, the settlers returned to the place.

The Israeli army has built an entire Arab village in the Negev for training purposes. Somebody joked this week that the army has also built this outpost and manned it with soldiers disguised as settlers, so it can be demolished every time there is pressure from America. Afterwards the soldiers build it up again, ready for use the next time pressure is exerted.

REFUSAL TO freeze the settlements means refusal to accept the two-state solution. Instead, Netanyahu juggled with empty slogans. He spoke about "two peoples living together in peace", but refused to speak about a Palestinian state. One of his aides called the demand for two states a "childish game".

But this is not a childish game at all. It has already been proven that negotiations, the aim of which has not been defined in advance, do not lead anywhere. The Oslo agreement collapsed for precisely this reason. Netanyahu hopes that the next round of negotiations will also founder because of this. He has not presented a plan of his own. Not because he has no plan, but because he knows that nobody would accept it.

Netanyahu's plan is: total Israeli control over all the country between the Mediterranean Sea and the Jordan River. Jewish settlements everywhere. Limited self-government
for a number of Palestinian enclaves with a dense Palestinian population, which will be surrounded by settlements. All of Jerusalem to remain part of Israel. Not a single Palestinian refugee to return to the territory of Israel.

This merchandise will find no buyers in the whole wide world. So Netanyahu, a professional salesman, tries to wrap it in an attractive package.For example: the Palestinians will "govern themselves". Where exactly? Where will the borders run? He has already pronounced that the Palestinians cannot have control over "their airspace or their border crossings". A state without a military and without control over its airspace and border crossings – that looks suspiciously like the Bantustans of the late racist apartheid regime in South Africa.

I would not be surprised if at some point in the future Netanyahu starts to call these native reservations "a Palestinian state". In the meanwhile he tries to gain time and postpone the negotiations as long as possible. He demands that the Palestinians recognize Israel as 'the state of the Jewish people", expecting and hoping that they will reject this with both hands. And indeed, accepting it would mean giving up in advance their main card – the refugee issue – and also sticking a knife in the back of the 1.5 million Palestinians who are citizens of Israel.

Netanyahu is ready to accept Obama's proposal to involve the Arab and other Muslim states in the peace process – an idea that has always been rigorously rejected by all Israel governments. But that is just one more of the rabbits that he will pull out of his hat from time to time in order to delay everything. Before dozens of Arab and perhaps more than fifty Muslim states decide whether to join the process, months, perhaps years will pass. And in the meantime, Netanyahu demands from them an advance payment in the form of normalization – which means that the entire Arab and Muslim world would give up their only card without getting anything in return. Pure baksheesh. That is Netanyahu's working plan.

DOES OBAMA have a peace plan of his own? If one puts all his statements of the last few days together, it seems that he has. When he speaks about "two states for two peoples", he practically accepts the peace plan that has by now become a world-wide consensus: as the "parameters" put forward by Bill Clinton in his last days in office, as the core of the Saudi peace proposal and as the peace plans of the Israeli peace movement (the draft peace agreement of Gush Shalom, the Geneva initiative, the Ayalon-Nusseibeh statement and more.)

In short: a sovereign and viable State of Palestine side by side with Israel, the pre-1967 borders with minor and agreed exchanges of territory, the dismantling of all the settlements that will not be joined to Israel in the territory exchanges, East Jerusalem as the capital of Palestine and West Jerusalem as the capital of Israel, a mutually acceptable solution to the refugee problem, a safe passage between the West Bank and the Gaza Strip, mutual security arrangements.

IN THE MEANTIME, throughout the world there is a growing consensus that the only way to get the wheels of peace moving again is for Obama to publish his peace plan and call upon both sides to accept it. If need be, in popular referendums.

He could do this in the speech he is due to deliver in two weeks time in Cairo, during his first presidential trip to the Middle East. Not by accident, he will not come to Israel during this trip, something that is almost unprecedented for a US president.

To do this, he must be ready to take on the powerful Israeli lobby. It seems that he is ready for that. The last president who dared to do this was Dwight D. Eisenhower, who compelled Israel to give back the Sinai straight after the 1956 war. "Ike" was so popular that he was not afraid of the lobby. Obama is no less popular, and perhaps he will dare, too. As "Teddy" Roosevelt indicated: when you have a big stick, you don't have to wave it, you can afford to speak softly. I hope Obama will indeed speak softly – but clearly and unambiguously.

THE REAL NATIONAL SECURITY THREAT:

Anonymous FBI 'sources,' speaking to LA Times and New York Times reporters, have claimed that Israel, mossad, & AIPAC runs a larger espionage operation in, and against, the United States than any other foreign country except Russia. ---

Israel, Mossad, and AIPAC provides a constant flow of information gathered by Israeli intelligence to the United States, the training of American soldiers by their very experienced Israeli counterparts in counter—terrorist and counterinsurgency tactics, torture technics, and logistical support for our troops in Iraq. And most importantly supplied the false intelligence used by the Bush administration to pre- emptively strike Iraq.

This foreign lobby (AIPAC) and the espionage involved with Israel puts the national security of the United States, in the gravest jeopardy, yet our government officials continue to take the bribes, listen to their think tanks, and continue appointments of members to important positions.

Israeli engineers have developed much of the American military's cutting—edge weapons technology in recent years that in itself makes no sense. AIPAC is discredited in the eyes of the American public as a nest of spies, but our officials ignore our concerns.

Thousands of Palestinians have marked 'Nakba Day', the 61st anniversary of Israeli occupation of Palestine, calling for the Palestinian refugees' right of return.

How long will we continue to support the Israeli atrocities? How long will we continue to allow our officials to cow-down? How long will we allow our congress to be influenced by foreign interest, our financial institutions, media, and entertainment industries to be monopolized by the same foreign interest??

Will anyone demand the type of investigations required to prove such. In reality nothing is more important then taking back our Country. Not one party or the other, but America & American. NOT Israel, Mossad, AIPAC, or any other FOREIGN interest lobby.

Now the same idiots want us to go to WAR with Iran for their interest. OUR young men & women sacrifice life or limb again for such a fascist regime. Stand up and say HELL no. Recognize who is the real National Security threat to the USA.

Does AIPAC engage in espionage against the United States? Does Israel? What does the FBI really know??

AIPAC IS NOT ABOVE THE LAW, OR ARE THEY??

Prosecutors and investigators had used FBI wiretaps to pursue Rosen and Weissman for at least five years, building a complex case that involved secret court hearings and dozens of legal filings and rulings. The two men were charged in 2005 with conspiring to obtain classified information -- about topics including al-Qaeda and U.S. forces in Iraq -- and pass it to the Israeli government and journalists from The Washington Post and other news organizations.

Gary Wasserman, a professor of government at Georgetown University who is writing a book about the case, said he was not surprised that

AIPAC was pleased by the proposed dismissal. A trial, he added, "would have provoked a lot of public discussion about how they worked." It is more fact then fiction that a foreign lobby called AIPAC, controls the THINK TANKS Washington takes most of their advice & campaign money from.

Not a word about the situation in any major newspaper today. Has AIPAC got all of them tied up in their pocket? Has it officially come to a point where it is treason to criticise Israel and their genocidal policies?

US congressional leaders and the most powerful pro-Israel lobby group in the US, AIPAC, are attempting to forestall a significant shift in the White House's Middle East policy. The American Israel Public Affairs Committee (Aipac) this week sent hundreds of lobbyists to urge members of Congress to sign a letter to Obama. The letter written by two House of Representative leaders, calls for Israel to be allowed, to set the pace of negotiations.

The lobbying came despite critics saying Netanyahu has consistently failed to commit himself to the creation of a Palestinian state. The letter calls for the maintenance of the status quo, with an emphasis on Palestinian institution-building before there can be an end to Israeli occupation.

Aipac wields considerable influence in the US Congress. Its critics say that what amounts to bullying pressure tactics has narrowed the room for debate about Israel, and claim the group has played a leading role in unseating some members of Congress who were critical of the Jewish state's policies. It is time for the American people to stand-up and get rid of the foreign lobbies, and stink tanks that have created such a mess in OUR capitol, and political system. Clear the halls of congress of the corruption and foreign interest.

Not all, but 75% of the corrupt with-in our government-- are Republican. WHY! Would any moral, intelligent, ethical, citizen of the USA ever vote for a Republican again? Their agenda is not for the good of us average Americans. Or any one else for that matter.

Until the Republican leadership recognizes the "Rule of Law", and they insist on prosecuting the violations and out right criminal activity conducted over the past eight years. They will only be able to win appointments for Dog Catcher, and then they will need to be unopposed. Republican-----The party of hypocrisy.

WE NEED REAL CHANGE FROM OUR FOREIGN POLICIES!!

First of all, I want to apologize to all the good women who are engaged in the world's oldest profession. I recently described Shimon Peres as a political prostitute. One of my female readers has protested vigorously. Prostitutes, she pointed out, earn their money honestly. They deliver what they promise.

Our president, on the other hand, only tells the truth by accident. He is a political impostor and a political sham. To him, too, apply Winston Churchill's words about a former Prime Minister: "The Right Honorable gentleman sometimes stumbles upon the truth, but he always hurries on as if nothing has happened." Or the words of former minister Amnon Rubinstein about Ariel Sharon: "He blushes when he tells the truth."

Like a traveling salesman offering a counterfeit product, Peres is now peddling the merchandise called Binyamin Netanyahu. He presents to the world a Netanyahu we have never known: a peacemaker, the epitome of truthfulness, a man with no other ambition than to go down in history as the founder of the State of Palestine. A Righteous Jew to outshine all Righteous Gentiles. HOWEVER, ALL these lies are nothing compared to trivializing the Holocaust. In some countries, that is a criminal offense, punishable by prison. The trivializing has many guises. For example: the assertion that the gas chambers never existed. Or: that not six million Jews were killed, but only six hundred thousand. But the most dangerous form of minimizing is the comparison of the Holocaust to passing events, thus turning it into "a detail of history", as Jean-Marie Le-Pen infamously put it. This week, Shimon Peres committed exactly this crime.

Like a lackey walking in front of the king, strewing flowers on the road, Peres flew to the US to prepare the ground for Netanyahu's coming visit. He imposed himself on a reluctant Barack Obama, who had no choice but to receive him.

Posing as a new Winston Churchill, the man who warned the world against the rise of Nazi Germany, he informed Obama with solemn bombast: "As Jews we cannot but compare Iran to Nazi Germany."

About this sentence at least three things must be said: (a) it is untrue, (b) it trivializes the Holocaust, and (c) it reflects a catastrophic policy.

DOES IRAN really resemble Nazi Germany?

I don't like the regime there. As a person who insists on total separation between state and religion, I oppose any regime based on religion – in Iran, in Israel or in any other country. Also, I don't like politicians like Mahmoud Ahmadinejad. I am allergic to leaders who stand on balconies and declaim to the masses below. I detest demagogues who appeal to the base instincts of hatred and fear. Alas, Ahmadinejad is not the only leader of this type. Indeed, the world is full of them; some are among the staunchest supporters of the Israeli government. In Israel, too, we do not lack this sort.

But Iran is not a fascist state. According to the evidence, there is quite a lot of freedom there, including freedom of expression. Ahmadinejad is not the only candidate for president in the present election campaign. There are a number of others, some more radical, some less. Nor is Iran an anti-Semitic state. A Jewish community, whose members are refusing to emigrate, is living there comfortably enough. It enjoys religious freedom and has a representative in parliament. Even if we take such reports with a grain of salt, it is clear that the Jews in Iran are not being persecuted like the Jews in Nazi Germany.

And, most important: Iran is not an aggressive country. It has not attacked its neighbors for centuries. The long and bloody Iraq-Iran war was started by Saddam Hussein. It may be remembered that at the time

Israel (contrary to the US) supported the Iranian side and supplied it with arms. (One such transaction was accidentally disclosed in the Irangate affair.) Before the Khomeini revolution, Iran was our most important ally in the region.

Ahmadinejad hates Israel. But it has been denied that he has threatened to annihilate Israel. It appears that the crucial sentence in his famous speech was mistranslated: he did not declare his determination to wipe Israel off the map, but expressed the opinion that Israel will disappear from the map.

Frankly, I don't think that there is such a great difference between the two versions. When the leader of a big country predicts that my state will disappear, that makes me worry. When that country appears to do everything possible to produce a nuclear bomb that worries me even more. I draw conclusions, but about that later.

Moreover, Ahmadinejad – unlike Hitler – is not the supreme leader of his country. He is subject to the real leadership, composed of clerics. All the signs indicate that this is not a group of adventurers. On the contrary, they are very balanced, sophisticated and prudent. Now they are cautiously feeling their way towards dialogue with the US, trying to reach an accord without sacrificing their regional ambitions, which are quite normal.

In brief, the speeches of one demagogic leader do not turn a country into Nazi Germany. Iran is not a mad country. It has no real interests in Israel/Palestine. Its interests are focused on the Persian Gulf area, and it wants to increase its influence throughout the Arab and Muslim world. Its relations with Syria, Hizbullah and Hamas mostly serve this purpose, and so does the anti-Israeli incitement of Ahmadinejad.

In brief, the comparison of Iran to Nazi Germany lacks a factual basis. From the Jewish point of view, the comparison is even more objectionable.

The Holocaust was a unique crime. True, the 20th century has seen other terrible acts of genocide, but they did not resemble the Shoa. In the Ottoman Empire, a horrifying massacre of the Armenian citizens took place, which amounted to genocide. Hitler himself mentioned it, saying that the annihilation of the Jews would similarly be forgotten. Stalin killed millions of Soviet citizens in the name of a monstrous ideology, which had started as a humanist creed. So did Pot Pol, who killed millions in order to change society for the better. In Rwanda, members of one tribe slaughtered the members of another. And, alas, the list goes on.

But Nazi Germany was unique in employing the instruments of a modern industrial society in order to eliminate helpless minorities (let's not forget the Roma, those with disabilities and the homosexuals) in a prolonged, planned and highly organized process, with the participation of all the organs of the state. If the Nazi regime had not been overthrown by war, Hitler would have continued with the annihilation of many more millions of Poles, Ukrainians and Russians.

Nothing like that can reasonably be expected to happen in Iran. Neither the ideology, nor the composition of the regime nor any other indication leads in that direction. As far as its growing nuclear capabilities are concerned – the Israeli deterrent power will prevent any such thought from arising. (Let's not forget that the only country ever to use nuclear bombs in war was our friend, the USA.)

Nothing that is happening in the world today resembles the Shoa, in which six million Jews were wiped out. The Palestinians did not kill six million Israelis, and we did not kill six million Palestinians. Comparing the Arabs to the Nazis is no less odious than comparing the Israelis to the Nazis. Many terrible things have been and are being committed in our name – but they are as far from the deeds of the Nazis as the earth is from distant galaxies. Any such comparison for the sake of some fleeting propaganda advantage is trivializing the Holocaust and its perpetrators. If the Nazis were not worse than the Ayatollahs, then the Shoa was not so terrible, after all.

In all my contacts with Palestinian leaders, including Yasser Arafat, I have always advised them to avoid this upsetting comparison. This would also be good advice for our own leaders.

DOES THE comparison of Iran to Nazi Germany serve Israeli interests? Iran is there. It was our ally in the past, and may be our ally again in the future. Leaders come and go, but geopolitical interests are more or less constant. Ahmadinejad may be replaced by a leader who will see Iranian interests in a different light.

The nuclear threat to Israel will not disappear – not after a (bad) speech by Peres nor after a (good) speech by Netanyahu. All over the region, nuclear installations will pop up. This process cannot be stopped. We all need nuclear energy to desalinate water and to produce electricity without destroying the environment. As an Israeli professor, a former employee in the nuclear center at Dimona, said this week: we must reconsider our nuclear policy. It may well be to our advantage to accept the demand of the American spokeswoman that Israel (as well as India and Pakistan) join the Nuclear Nonproliferation Treaty and a regime of strict supervision.

President Barack Obama is now saying to Israel: Put an end to the Israeli-Palestinian conflict. That is a precondition for the elimination of the threat to Israel. When the Palestinians, and the entire Arab world, make peace with Israel – Iran will not be able to exploit the conflict for the furthering of its interests. We were saying this, by the way, many years ago.

The refusal of Netanyahu-Lieberman-Barak to accept this demand shows the insincerity of their arguments about Iran. If they really believed that Iran posed an existential menace, they would hurry to dismantle the settlements, demolish the outposts and make peace. That would, after all, be a small price to pay for the elimination of an existential danger. Their refusal proves that the entire existential story is a bluff.

And concerning the comparison of Iran to Nazi Germany – it is as convincing as the comparison of Shimon Peres to Sir Winston.

EXCLUSIVE:

President Obama's efforts to curb the spread of nuclear weapons threaten to expose and derail a 40-year-old secret U.S. agreement to shield Israel's nuclear weapons from international scrutiny, former and current U.S. and Israeli officials and nuclear specialists say. The issue will likely come to a head when Israeli Prime Minister Benjamin Netanyahu meets with Mr. Obama on May 18 in Washington. Mr. Netanyahu is expected to seek assurances from Mr. Obama that he will uphold the U.S. commitment and will not trade Israeli nuclear concessions for Iranian ones.

Assistant Secretary of State Rose Gottemoeller, speaking Tuesday at a U.N. meeting on the nuclear Non-Proliferation Treaty (NPT), said Israel should join the treaty, which would require Israel to declare and relinquish its nuclear arsenal.

"Universal adherence to the NPT itself, including by India, Israel, Pakistan and North Korea, ... remains a fundamental objective of the United States," Ms. Gottemoeller told the meeting, according to Reuters.

RELATED MATERIAL:

- ♦ America has protected Israeli nuke program for 40 years
- ♦ Click here to see the National Security Archives at George Washington University.
- ♦ Click here to download the May 4 statement by Iran's Deputy Foreign Minister at the Third Session of the Preparatory Committee of 2010 NPT Review Conference.
- ♦ Click here to download a PDF of a memo that has been declassified by the Nixon library.

She declined to say, however, whether the Obama administration would press Israel to join the treaty. A senior White House official said the administration considered the nuclear programs of Israel and Iran to be unrelated "apples and oranges." Asked by The Washington Times whether the administration would press Israel to join the NPT, the official said, "We support universal adherence to the NPT. [It] remains a long-term goal."

The official spoke on the condition of anonymity because of the sensitivity of the issue.

Avner Cohen, author of "Israel and the Bomb" and the leading expert outside the Israeli government on the history of Israel's nuclear program, said Mr. Obama's "upcoming meeting with Netanyahu, due to the impending discussions with Iran, will be a platform for Israel to ask for reassurances that old understandings on the nuclear issue are still valid."

For the past 40 years, Israel and the U.S. have kept quiet about an Israeli nuclear arsenal that is now estimated at 80 to 200 weapons. Israel has promised not to test nuclear weapons while the U.S. has not pressed Israel to sign the nuclear NPT, which permits only five countries - the U.S., France, Britain, China and Russia - to have nuclear arms.

The U.S. also has opposed most regional calls for a "nuclear-free Middle East." The accord was forged at a summit between Israeli Prime Minister Golda Meir and President Nixon on Sept. 25, 1969, according to recently released documents, but remains so secret that there is no explicit record of it. Mr. Cohen has referred to the deal as "don't ask, don't tell," because it commits both the U.S. and Israel never to acknowledge in public Israels nuclear arsenal. When asked what the Obama administration's position was on the 1969 understanding, the senior White House official offered no comment. Over the years, demands for Israel to come clean have multiplied.

The Iran factor

Iranian leaders have long complained about being subjected to a double standard that allows non-NPT members India and Pakistan, as well as Israel, to maintain and even increase their nuclear arsenals but sanctions Tehran, an NPT member, for not cooperating fully with the International Atomic Energy Agency (IAEA), the U.N. nuclear watchdog.

On Monday, Iranian Deputy Foreign MinisterMohammad Ali Hosseini told a U.N. meeting preparing for a major review of the NPT next year that nuclear cooperation by the U.S., France and Britain with Israel is "in total disregard with the obligations under the treaty and commitments undertaken in 1995 and 2000, and a source of real concern for the international community, especially the parties to the treaty in the Middle East."

The Obama administration is seeking talks with Iran on its nuclear program and has dropped a precondition for negotiations that Iran first suspend its uranium enrichment program. "What the Israelis sense, rightly, is that Obama wants to do something new on Iran and this may very well involve doing something new about Israel's program," said Henry Sokolski, executive director of the Nuclear Nonproliferation Policy Education Center, a Washington think tank.

AMERICA: Demand that our President and CONGRESS stop the double standard.
Israel has not confirmed that it has nuclear weapons and officially maintains that it will not be the first country to introduce nuclear weapons into the Middle East. Yet the existence of Israeli nuclear weapons is a "public secret" by now due to the declassification of large numbers of formerly highly classified US government documents which show that the United States by 1975 was convinced that Israel had nuclear weapons.

There followed two decades in which the United States, through a combination of benign neglect, erroneous analysis, and successful Israeli deception, failed to discern first the details of Israel's nuclear program. As early as 8 December 1960, the CIA issued a report outlining Dimona's implications for nuclear proliferation, and the CIA station in Tel Aviv had determined by the mid-1960s that the Israeli nuclear weapons program was an established and irreversible fact. By the late 1990s the U.S. Intelligence Community estimated that Israel possessed between 75-130 weapons, based on production estimates. The stockpile would certainly include warheads for mobile Jericho-1 and Jericho-2 missiles, as well as bombs for Israeli aircraft, and may include other tactical nuclear weapons of various types. Some published estimates even claimed that Israel might have as many as 400 nuclear weapons by the late 1990s. We believe these numbers are exaggerated, and that Israel's nuclear weapons inventory may include less than 100 nuclear weapons. Stockpiled plutonium could be used to build additional weapons if so decided. DO WE REALLY KNOW OUR ALLIES AND ENEMIES??

2006 & 2008 MANDATES CHANGE.

THE AMERICAN PEOPLE HAVE DEMANDED "CHANGE", MEANING REFORM, AND GOVERNMENT BY THE PEOPLE.

What have we gotten for change?
Pennies, nichols, dimes and quarters. Not many of those.

WHY WE NEED A THIRD PARTY--renege on promise to US!!

Breaking: US House backs $96.7 bln bill for Iraq, Afghan, Pakistan wars 14 May 2009 The U.S. House of Representatives on Thursday approved a $96.7 billion measure to fund the wars in Iraq and Afghanistan through Sept. 30 as well as rush critical economic and security aid [?] to Pakistan. The biggest chunk is $47.7 billion to support military operations in Iraq and Afghanistan through Sept. 30. Obama had originally requested in total $84.3 billion. It also includes $1 billion for Pakistan as it tries to fight militant Taliban 'insurgents.'
U.N. rights chief urges Obama to prosecute torturers 14 May 2009 The U.N. High Commissioner for Human Rights on Thursday welcomed the election of the United States to the top United Nations rights forum and urged it to prosecute those accused of torture and other abuses. Navi Pillay said Washington should investigate all U.S. renditions of terrorism suspects and ensure any interrogators who mistreated them are brought to justice for violating an international ban on torture.

Speaker Pelosi: CIA, Bush team misled on water boarding 14 May 2009 Under strong attack from Republicans, the leader of the U.S. House of Representatives, Speaker Nancy Pelosi (D-Calf.), accused the CIA and

Bush administration of misleading her about water boarding detainees and sharply rebutted claims she was complicit in its use. "To the contrary ... we were told explicitly that water boarding was not being used," she said, referring to a formal CIA briefing she received in late 2002.

Pelosi accuses CIA of misleading her on use of water boarding 14 May 2009 House Speaker Nancy Pelosi accused CIA officials Thursday of misleading her in 2002 about the use of "enhanced interrogation techniques" such as water boarding, which simulates drowning and has been described by critics as torture. Pelosi reiterated an earlier claim that she was briefed on such techniques only once -- in September 2002 -- and that she was told at the time that the techniques were not being used.

Indefinite Detention Weighed 14 May 2009 The Obama administration [soon to be dubbed 'regime' by the CLG] is weighing plans to detain some terror suspects on U.S. soil indefinitely and without trial -- as part of a plan to retool military tribunal trials that were conducted for prisoners held in Guantanamo Bay, Cuba. The proposal is being floated with members of Congress... Sen. Lindsay Graham (R., S.C.), who met this week with White House Counsel Greg Craig to discuss the administration's plans, said among the proposals being studied is seeking authority for indefinite detentions, with the imprimatur of some type of national-security court.

'It's perfectly Orwellian... It's just more evidence that this Administration is becoming the greatest bait-and-switch in history. He's morphing into his predecessor.' --Law Professor Jonathan Turley, referring to Barack Obama 13 May 2009 (MSNBC)

Obama refuses to publicize army abuse photos 13 May 2009 US President Barack Obama has refused the release of photographs of detainee abuse in Iraq and Afghanistan. President Obama has told reporters that while the photos depict behaviour that did not conform with US Army rules of conduct, the people responsible for the offences have been dealt with.

Obama bows to Republican right and military on torture photos By Bill Van Auken 14 May 2009 The Obama administration's decision Wednesday to renege on its promise to comply with a court order and release photographs of US personnel torturing detainees in Iraq and Afghanistan represents another capitulation by his administration to mounting pressure from the right and the military-intelligence apparatus... He claimed that the images are "not particularly sensational" and "would not add any additional benefit to our understanding of what was carried out in the past by a small number of individuals." Obama failed to explain what makes the US president the arbiter of what is of "benefit to our understanding."

Quick action! Tell President Obama you support transparency and accountability. (ACLU) 13 May 2009 The very fact that photos of torture and abuse exist, only underscores the need for transparency, accountability and for a full investigation of crimes committed. The President... needs to hear from concerned citizens like you. Join the ACLU in calling on President Obama to put the full weight of his leadership behind our call for transparency and accountability. (Petition)

Reid says no plan no Guantanamo closure 14 May 2009 The US Senate will not provide funding to close the Guantanamo Bay prison facility until President Barack Obama provides a concrete proposal on doing so. "There will be nothing happening until a plan comes from the president," Majority Leader, Harry Reid, told reporters on Thursday. The Senate Appropriations Committee is considering Obama's request for USD 80m to shutter the controversial detention center by January 22, 2010, and attach strict conditions to its closing.

The CIA is hiring: Experienced Torturers needed - (no Muslims need apply) By Jack Rabbit 13 May 2009 Take a look at this article regarding torture of prisoners in the custody of MY GOVERNMENT! From the article: "Who the hell authorizes these things?" Soufan reportedly asked the chief CIA officer in Thailand, as Mitchell began stripping the prisoner and blasting him with music from the Red Hot Chili Peppers." So here I sit, with only news articles to tell me what my government is up to. (That would be torture.) Thankfully there are some brave souls willing to become "whistleblowers" because their conscience prevents restful sleep knowing torture is going on at the hands of the government of the land of the free and the home of the brave.

60-year-old Army soldier is oldest killed in Iraq -- Ariz. man was Vietnam vet who decided to re-enlist after 9/11 attacks 14 May 2009 A 60-year-old Vietnam War veteran who was killed by a roadside bomb in Iraq has become the oldest Army soldier to die in that conflict, the military said Thursday. An Associated Press database of soldiers killed in Iraq and Afghanistan shows that Maj. Steven Hutchison, of Scottsdale, Ariz., is the oldest member of any service branch killed since the wars broke out.

Pirate attacks pass 2008 mark 14 May 2009 Piracy attacks off the Somali coast since January have surpassed the number for all of 2008, according to the International Maritime Bureau. The Piracy Reporting Center at IMB recorded 111 piracy incidents in 2008 in the Gulf of Aden and off the Somali coast. So far this year, the center has documented 114 attempted attacks, including 29 successful hijackings, the IMB reported. [See: Somali pirates guided by London intelligence team, report says 11 May 2009.]

Singapore Air Force arrives in Mountain Home 13 May 2009 The world outside Idaho got a little bit smaller Wednesday, as four F-15SG fighter jets flown from St. Louis by the Republic of Singapore Air Force landed between rainstorms at Mountain Home Air Force Base. Greeted by a cheering crowd of more than 100 military personnel from both Singapore and the U.S., the four jets are the first of as many as 10 that will call the airbase home for at least the next 20 years. More than 300 active-duty and support personnel will make up the 428th Fighter Squadron and train alongside American pilots as part of a partnership between the two countries - though they will not fly on missions.

Nuclear Surety Inspection begins at Minot AFB 14 May 2009 A Nuclear Surety Inspection was initiated Wednesday at Minot Air Force Base. The inspection team is led by a senior officer representative from the Air Combat Command Inspector General's office with oversight provided by representatives from the Air Force Inspection Agency and the office of the Secretary of the Air Force. This no-notice inspection is expected to conclude May 22. [A 'no-notice' inspection? Look for the Minot AFB Clandestine Nukes 'Oddities' page to grow in the aftermath of that one. --LRP]

Quick action! Keep your promise, President Obama --Tell the President to end "Don't Ask, Don't Tell" policy and not fire Lt. Dan Choi (Courage Campaign) 14 May 2009 Lt. Dan Choi, from Orange County, California, is a graduate of the U.S. Military Academy at West Point and an Iraq War veteran. Last March he went on Rachel Maddow's show and spoke three truthful words: "I am gay." As a result Lt. Choi received a letter from the Army on April 23 discharging him for violating the "Don't Ask, Don't Tell" policy... Lt. Choi is fighting to stay in the military and ensure that no other soldier is ever again discharged as a result of "Don't Ask, Don't Tell." President Obama did not create this policy. But he now has the opportunity to keep his promise and allow gay and lesbian soldiers to serve openly in the military. It's the right thing to do -- for justice and for national security. (Petition)

Britain has freed more than half of those arrested as terrorism suspects 14 May 2009 More than half of those arrested on suspicion of terrorism-related offenses in Britain since Sept. 11, 2001, have been freed without being charged, according to government statistics released Wednesday. Of the 1,471 people detained, 521 were charged and 196 of those were convicted of terrorism-related charges, the British Home Office survey shows; 819 were released without being charged. Some were charged with offenses not related to terrorism, such as theft, fraud or an expired visa. The report does not say how many of those were convicted.

Scouts Train to Fight Terrorists, and More --In a competition in Arizona, one role-player wore traditional Arab dress. 14 May 2009 But the more than 2,000 law enforcement posts across the country are the Explorers' most popular, accounting for 35,000 of the group's 145,000 members, said John Anthony, national director of Learning for Life. Since the attacks of Sept. 11, 2001, and the wars in Iraq and Afghanistan, many posts have taken on an emphasis of fighting terrorism and other less conventional threats... The law enforcement posts are restricted to those ages 14 to 21 who have a C average, but there seems to be some wiggle room. [Stupid little fascists with guns - just what we need.]

San Mateo man with tuberculosis faces charge for disobeying quarantine --His resistance to complying with doctors prompted a formal public health order May 6 from county health officer Dr. Scott Morrow. 12 May 2009 A 60-year-old man who was being treated for tuberculosis at Kaiser Permanente Medical Center in Redwood City faces a criminal charge for repeatedly disobeying a quarantine order from the San Mateo County Health Department. Charles Dvorak was diagnosed with contagious tuberculosis after being admitted to the hospital April 27 for a severe cough.

Scientist: Swine Flu Could Have Come From Bio-Experiment Lab --World Health Organization Investigates Claims by Australian Scientist 14 May 2009 An Australian researcher claims the swine flu, which has killed at least 64 people so far, might not be a mutation that occurred naturally but a man-made product of genetic experiments accidentally leaked from a laboratory. Adrian Gibbs, a scientist on the team that was behind the development of Tamiflu, says in a report he is submitting today that swine flu might have been created using eggs to grow viruses and make new vaccines, and could have been accidentally [purposefully] leaked to the general public.

Scientist arrested for smuggling vials used in Ebola research into US --Yao told US border guards he was taking them to his new job with the National Institutes of Health at the Biodefense Research Laboratory in Bethesda, MD. 13 May 2009 A Canadian scientist has been arrested for smuggling 22 vials stolen from Canada's National Microbiology Lab, used in Ebola and HIV research, into the United States, Canadian and US officials said Wednesday. Konan Michel Yao "was taken into custody" while crossing the border from Manitoba province into the western US state of North Dakota on May 5, said a spokeswoman for the Public Health Agency of Canada, which operates the lab. According to US prosecutor Lynn Jordheim, Yao was detained for carrying unidentified biological materials in vials wrapped in aluminum foil inside a glove and packaged in a plastic bag, along with electrical wires, in the trunk of his car.

China seeks passengers with exposure to new A/H1N1 flu case 14 May 2009 China's Ministry of Health confirmed Wednesday a Shandong man has tested positive for the A/H1N1 flu and authorities are seeking plane and train passengers who had exposure to the man. The case, the second of its kind on the Chinese mainland, involved a 19-year-old student who arrived in Beijing from Canada May 8 and traveled to Jinan, provincial capital of Shandong, three days later in a train labeled D41.

NYC closing schools to deal with big flu outbreak 14 May 2009 New York City has closed three schools in response to a swine flu outbreak that has left one staff member in critical condition and sent hundreds of kids home with flu symptoms, in a flare-up of the deadly virus that sent shock waves through the world last month.

No. of new influenza patients tops 6,000 worldwide; 65 dead 14 May 2009 The number of people infected with a new strain of influenza has topped 6,000 in 35 countries and territories around the globe as of early Thursday, according to government announcements and media reports. The number of people infected with the H1N1 virus has come to 6,465.

A pandemic strategy, that is worse then swine-flu.
The finest group of "MORRONS"

There are antiviral medicines you can take to prevent or treat swine flu. There is no vaccine available right now to protect against a pandemic strategy of the following. The finest group of Diplomats and political advisors the Republican Party can gather to push their coming agenda. "Make sure Obama fails at all cost". 1. Bobby Jindal 2. Sarah Palin 3. Michael Steel 4. Rush Limbaugh 5. Bill O'Reilly 6. George Will 7. Ann Coulter 8. Carl Rove 9. Joe "Lie"berman 10. Pat Robertson 11. John McCain 12. Mitch McConnell 13. Newt Gingrich A team dedicated to the party regardless of the culture of corruption and criminal activity for the last 25 years. When the financial rewards, outweighs any values.

CRUSH RUSH THE LUSH, FLUSH HIM OUT OF HERE! Please, take your friends with you, thanks the tax-payers. IMPORTANT TO NOTE: Remember when you go to the voting booth: The Bankers that helped cause the mess--Are Republican. The Wall Street Brokers that ripped you off--Are Republican. The Oil companies, with excessive profits from you--Are Republican. The drug companies with excessive Profits--Are Republican. The companies that out-sourced your jobs--Are Republican. The Insurance Companies that lobby against Health Care reform are of course--Republican. The War profiteers, no bid contractors--Are Republican. Not all, but 75% of the corrupt with-in our government-- are Republican. WHY! Would any moral, intelligent, ethical, citizen of the USA ever vote for a Republican again? Their agenda is not for the good of us average Americans, nor any one else, for that matter.

Until the Republican leadership recognizes the "Rule of Law", and they insist on prosecuting the violations and out right criminal activity conducted over the past
eight years . They will only be able to win appointments for Dog Catcher, and then they will need to be unopposed.

Detroit fund sues Halliburton, KBR 14 May 2009 The Detroit Policemen & Firemen Retirement System filed a lawsuit in U.S. District Court in Houston today against oil field services provider Halliburton Co. and its one-time subsidiary KBR Inc., accusing Halliburton's board of directors of breach of fiduciary duty for misdeeds and corruption resulting in damage to investors' holdings. The lawsuit, brought on behalf of the retirement system by Wilmington, Del.-based law firm Grant & Eisenhofer P.A. and Houston-based Lanier Law Firm, names current and former directors of Halliburton [Cheney?] as defendants.

'The saver is going to start rebelling.' Billionaire Rupert Says Crisis May Provoke Unrest, Inflation Share 14 May 2009 South African billionaire Johann Rupert said the financial crisis may lead to inflation and social unrest as savers find they're too poor to retire, while pension-fund managers deserve to be jailed for incompetence. Rupert, speaking at the annual presentation for Cie. Financiere Richemont SA, the luxury-goods company he controls, said he doesn't see any "green shoots" of economic recovery... Rupert told analysts at the meeting that they're too young to remember Red Brigade terrorism in Italy or the 1968 Paris uprisings, when the French state sent tanks into the streets. "Things can get volatile very quickly," he said.

Credit card reform bill slows in U.S. Senate 14 May 2009 A credit card reform bill that would ban arbitrary interest rate hikes remained stalled in the Senate on Thursday as Democratic and Republican leaders negotiated amendments to be offered by lawmakers. "I hope that we can pass it before we leave next Friday for our recess," Senate Democratic Leader Harry Reid told reporters.

US: Cuts in Social Security, Medicare to pay for bank bailouts By Tom Eley 14 May 2009 A government report made public Tuesday indicates that Social Security and Medicare will deplete their trust funds more quickly than previously forecast. This has sparked new demands from within the US financial elite for substantial cuts in the two entitlement programs, which pay retirement and medical benefits for tens of millions of working class Americans. The report was issued by the programs' trustees, a group of four Obama administration officials headed by Treasury Secretary Timothy Geithner.

Anger, sadness as ax falls on Chrysler dealers 14 May 2009 Dealers across the United States reacted with a mixture of anger and sadness on Thursday to word that bankrupt automaker Chrysler LLC plans to eliminate franchise agreements with them as part of its restructuring efforts. But most, even those surprised by the news, entertained little hope they could stop Chrysler from following through on the proposed closures...

Gov. proposes selling L.A. Coliseum, other properties to raise cash 14 May 2009 Gov. Arnold Schwarzenegger [R-Installed] wants to sell the Los Angeles Memorial Coliseum, San Quentin State Prison, the Orange County Fairgrounds and other state property to raise cash amid the state's growing fiscal crisis, according to a copy of a proposal reviewed by The Times. Sale of the properties, to be included in the governor's revised budget plan today, would raise between $600 million and $1 billion, although it would not provide financial relief for two to five years, according to the proposal.

Obama Delivers Inspirational Message to Class of 2009 14 May 2009 U.S. President Barack Obama has delivered his first commencement address since taking office, a speech to the graduating class of Arizona State University. President Obama told the graduating class at Arizona State that what drives them through life should not be money, celebrity or power, but a higher calling. Mr. Obama got a warm welcome in this university in the desert.

Pageant official quits over Miss California move 14 May 2009 In the latest twist in a scandal that has rocked an American beauty pageant, a former Miss USA [Shanna Moakler] has resigned as co-executive of the Miss California USA competition following owner Donald Trump's decision to let the state's controversial title holder keep her crown. Trump said that Carrie Prejean could retain her Miss California USA crown even after questions arose about semi-nude photographs taken of her as a teenager and her association with an anti-gay marriage group.

Previous lead stories: Obama U-turn on abuse photographs 13 May 2009 US President Barack Obama has changed his mind and will now attempt to block the publication of photographs showing the abuse of prisoners by US soldiers. The US government had previously said it would not fight a court ruling ordering the release of the pictures. Mr Obama now believes the release of the photos would make the job of US troops in Iraq and Afghanistan more difficult, White House officials said.

Obama threatens to limit US intel with UK over Guantanamo torture --Justice letter filed in court 12 May 2009 The Bush Obama administration says it may curtail Anglo-American intelligence sharing if the British High Court discloses new details of the treatment of a former Guantanamo prisoner. A court filing from the British Foreign Office released recently includes a letter from the U.S. government, identified as the "Obama administration's communication." At issue is whether the British courts will disclose a seven-paragraph summary of the treatment of Binyam Mohamed, a former prisoner who was released from Guantanamo Bay prison in February. Mr. Mohamed says he was tortured while in U.S., Pakistani and Moroccan custody.

U.S. military, Pakistan carrying out Predator drone missions together --The Pakistanis have yet to use the drones to shoot at suspected militants and are ambivalent over using U.S. equipment to fire on their own people. 12 May 2009 The U.S. military has begun flying armed Predator drones inside Pakistan and has given Pakistani officers significant control over targets, flight routes and decisions to launch attacks under a new joint operation, according to U.S. officials familiar with the program. Under the new partnership, U.S. military drones will be allowed for the first time to venture beyond the borders of Afghanistan under the direction of Pakistani military officials, who are working with American counterparts at a command center in Jalalabad, Afghanistan.

THE TRUTH IS COMING OUT:

The corruption in Washington between the Republican Party, AIPAC, and organized crime has become quite well known over the past few years.
It is also apparent that there are Democrats in Washington that are involved in the same syndicate, and take part in the insider corruption deals.
Now we can more then guess why immediately after the 2006 elections and mandate by the people,
Nancy Pelosi announced that Impeachment of Bush, Cheney, was OFF THE TABLE.
35 articles of impeachment are ignored by the speaker.
Her most recent fabrications are beginning to show the truth. Her connections to AIPAC, her supportive members in congress and their connections, are coming to light. We certainly need more sun-light into the leadership of both parties.
Her husband & real-estate tycoon Paul Pelosi was a New York investment banker turned San Francisco real estate developer. He is

president of Financial Leasing Services, a venture-capital company in San Francisco. He is a stock trader with millions in Microsoft, Amazon. com and AT&T. Net worth $90 million.

Pelosi overlooks Israel's brutal treatment of the Palestinians, and doesn't mention Israel's massive nuclear, chemical and biological weapons arsenal. Pelosi's view of Muslims versus Americans and Israelis is racist. According to Pelosi, the biggest danger to Israel today comes from Iran, whose nuclear ambitions, though still unproved, also threaten the US. She over-looks the facts of the atrocities by Israel, and over-looks the use of US weapons, and the possession of Nuclear weapons by Israel, much more then a desire to possess such.

Reform in government has to occur on both sides of the isle. They (both parties) will not seek change and reform It will take the people, a third party, and prosecutions from international agencies.

Pelosi has strong ties to a number of groups, including the American Israel Public Affairs Committee; she is a close friend of Amy Friedkin, a past AIPAC president.

This connection, as with many members of congress, posses the biggest threat to our National Security then any other. The foreign interest group has that much influence over our government. Follow the ear marks, budget request, and the votes and weed out the corrupt and connected.

Newt Gingrich's Skeleton Closet:

Mr. Family Values :(Republican & syndicate style ethics & Values)
Adultery: Callista Bisek. Anne Manning. The unnamed, "young volunteer". Are we missing anyone? Newt pressed his first wife to sign divorce papers while she was still in the hospital recovering from cancer surgery. He also graciously said "She isn't young enough or pretty enough to be the President's wife."

House Banking Scandal:
Newt Bounced 22 Checks. Remember the House Banking scandal, where so many congressmen wrote rubber checks on government

money? Newt hopes you don't, because he bounced 22 himself, which almost cost him reelection in 1992. His vote for the secret House pay raise, and the chauffeur who drove him around Washington in a Lincoln Town Car, didn't help.

The 1995 Murdoch Deal:
You probably heard something about Newt's book scandal. He was offered first $2.5 million, then $4.5 million by Harper Collins, a publishing company owned by Rupert Murdoch, who also owns the Fox TV network and newspapers and TV stations around the world. Murdoch has been having problems with a complaint by NBC that Fox is a foreign owned TV network, which is against US law.

The 1984 Book Deal
Murdoch's book deal wasn't the first lucrative and controversial book deal Newt engineered. In 1983 he established a limited partnership in Atlanta called COS Limited, which pulled together about two dozen of his biggest campaign contributors to finance his book.

GOPAC sleaze: Taxpayer subsidies for his partisan campaign course.
Newt in his political career was the king of using tax-payer subsidized donations for his personal and political purposes. He stooped so low as to hijack not one but two charities for poor inner city kids and use their donations for his personal goals.
GOPAC, Newt's longtime political action committee, was the centerpiece of a complex network of non-profit, and mostly tax exempt organizations that Newt has used to support himself and other conservative candidates. In an act of incredible hypocrisy, this crusader against taxes obtained taxpayer subsidies for his personal and political goals, by misusing these tax-exempt groups.

The Ethics Committee dropped its final charges against Gingrich not long before he resigned as speaker, despite finding that Gingrich had in fact violated one rule by repeatedly using a political consultant paid by GOPAC to develop the Republican political agenda, because there was no evidence he was continuing to do so.

Who Owns Him?

Rupert Murdoch (see book deal above)

Georgia's Richards family, owners of Southwire Corporate ($1.3 billion/year)

The Richards lent and donated money and office space to Gingrich from his earliest days in politics. They have given over $100,000, and Gingrich was the first recipient of donations from Southwire's PAC. By coincidence, Gingrich has changed from an environmentalist critic of Southwire to a staunch anti-environmentalist during that time. People with ties to Southwire were instrumental in two earlier lucrative book deals of Gingrich's in 1977 and 1984; the latter was investigated for ethical violations.

Ethics Committee Drops Last of 84 Charges Against Gingrich, By Curt Anderson (Associated Press), Washington Post, October 11, 1998, Page A13 .

Draft Dodger:

Though he relentlessly pushes military spending and talks like a bigtime hawk, Gingrich avoided the Vietnam War through a combination of student and family deferments. (He married one of his teachers at age 19.)

House Banking Scandal: Newt Bounced 22 Checks

Remember the House Banking scandal, where so many congressmen wrote rubber checks on government money? Newt hopes you don't, because he bounced 22 himself, which almost cost him reelection in 1992. His vote for the secret House pay raise, and the chauffeur who drove him around Washington in a Lincoln Town Car, didn't help.

Gingrich is touted as a possible Republican candidate in the next presidential campaign and has re-established himself as a top leader in the Republican party as the GOP struggles to redefine its identity and appeal to voters after electoral losses in the fall.

Gingrich at AIPAC

The American Israel Public Affairs Committee opted to end its plenary session (after a marathon of telemarketing-style donation appeals) with a speech from Newt Gingrich, introduced as a sort of prophet who been talking about Iran

Another politician, that is in their pocket.

Politicizing the Holocaust, equating the Obama administration with totalitarian communism, telling Jewish voters that the destruction of Israel by a Nazi-like threat is 'imminent'--such were the talking points in Newt Gingrich's speech to his political pocket book, AIPAC.

US LAW RELATING TO DUAL CITIZENSHIP:

1978 citizenship law amendments (Pub.L. 95-432)
1986 citizenship law amendments (Pub.L. 99-653)
1994 citizenship law amendments (Pub.L. 103-416)
2000 citizenship law amendments (Pub.L. 106-395)

No person with dual citizenship should be elected or appointed to any position with-in our government.

We have seen several changes in Foreign Policy for the last 30+ years. Such has not benefited the United States, but has benefited Foreign Interest.

Such change has come about due to the acceptance of foreign lobbies, think tanks, foreign professors as our experts, appointments to high level government positions, and the election of officials with dual interest instead of OUR
AMERICAN INTEREST being the priority.

We have seen our values & ethics deteriorate over the same period. It now becomes a real threat to our NATIONAL SECURITY.
LOOK CLOSE at who has nuclear weapons, are the aggressors of war with their neighbors, and has dual citizens serving with-in our government with foreign interest in mind. That for America is treason to us.

CIA's torture program:

Water boarding in July 2002:

US national security adviser Condoleezza Rice approved a CIA request to subject alleged al-Qaeda terrorist Abu Zubaydah to water boarding in July 2002. A few days later, the Justice Department approved the use of the torture technique in a secret memo that the Obama administration declassified last week. Rice's role was detailed in a narrative released today by the Senate Intelligence Committee. It provides the most detailed timeline yet for how the CIA's torture program was conceived and approved at the highest levels in the Bush White House.

Condoleezza Rice gave permission for the CIA to use water boarding techniques on the alleged al-Qaida terrorist Abu Zubaydah as early as July 2002, the first known official approval for the technique, according to a report released by the Senate intelligence committee yesterday. The revelation indicates that Rice, who at the time was national security adviser and went on to be secretary of state, played a greater role than she admitted [committed perjury] in written testimony last autumn.

A newly declassified narrative of the Bush regime's advice to the CIA on harsh interrogations shows that the small group of Justice Department lawyers who wrote memos authorizing torture were operating not on their own but with direction from top administration officials, including then-Vice President [sic] Dick Cheney and National Security Adviser Condoleezza Rice... Meanwhile, Sens. John McCain (R-AZ), Lindsey Graham (R-SC), and Joseph Lieberman (R-Israel) wrote to Obama urging him not to prosecute Bush officials who offered legal advice about CIA interrogations.

The Bush regime applied relentless pressure on interrogators to use harsh methods torture on prisoners in part to find evidence of cooperation between al Qaida and the late Iraqi president Saddam Hussein's government, according to a former senior U.S. intelligence official and a former Army psychiatrist. Such information would've provided a foundation for one of former President [sic] George W. Bush's main arguments for invading Iraq in 2003. In fact, no evidence has ever been found of operational ties between Osama bin Laden's terrorist network and Hussein's government.

Former President [sic] George W. Bush, Vice President [sic] Dick Cheney, National Security Adviser Condoleezza Rice, Defense Secretary Donald Rumsfeld, Secretary of State Colin Powell and other top Bush administration officials had detailed knowledge of the Central Intelligence Agency's torture tactics and approved them, according to a front-page article published Wednesday by the New York Times.

Mr. Cheney:

The public you keep trying to talk to believe you belong in jail. Get it, prison, behind bars. To stress the point so you might understand. We consider you and Rush to be America's top no.1 & no.2 "BUTT_ HOLES". How-ever we thank you both for taking the Republican Party into the "cess-pool" where it belongs. Please keep the Swine-Flu to yourselves.

Dear past Vice-President Mr. Cheney:
We are no longer playing Monopoly. There will not be any get out of jail free cards for you and other officials, past & present. We will return to a policy of the rule of law.

Colon Powell may have left the Republican Party, but HE remains an American with Americas interest . Not a fascist with foreign interest and corporate profits.

President Obama's Justice Department should indict and then prosecute decision maker's legal and executive who enabled and ordered torture. And Yoo should be at the top of this list. However, Attorney General Eric Holder has yet to take action against Bush administration torture leaders.

We must fight to bring justice to John Yoo on every front from appointing a special prosecutor, to taking away his license to practice law, to forcing the Philadelphia Inquirer to cancel his column.

We need a "CONSTITUTION PARTY" Third party to replace one or both others.
We need third parties more than ever.

HEALTH CARE REFORM:

The industry knows the same thing we do, and they don't like it: the only way to make reform work for patients and payers is to allow the option of a public insurance plan. Obama has committed to that in the past, but insurance companies are trying to talk him out of his pledge with these promises to cut some unspecified costs, some years in the future. We need to have OUR say about that. While we couldn't get into that room with the health industry lobbyists, we DO have access to a widely-read public forum: the local newspaper. You Can Set the Republican Party Straight Republicans like Governor Charlie Crist of Florida and Governor Arnold Schwarzenegger of California are working to help create a clean energy future for our country. But in Washington, too many Republican leaders continue to let Big Oil's lobbyists make their decisions for them and together, they're standing in the way of safe, renewable, American energy. Clean energy is the key to more jobs, a safer country, and a cooler planet – we simply can't afford to let Big Oil make this a partisan issue. Click here to tell the Republican Party in Washington to stop listening to Big Oil and to start being part of the clean energy solution. Don't Let Big Oil Get the Last Word Big Oil isn't just after Republicans. For the last week, the oil industry has been putting pressure on key members of Congress from both parties who sit on the Energy and Commerce Committee, the committee that will shape important clean energy legislation. BRING OUR TROOPS HOME: Nothing has changed the PEOPLES minds: The Obama administration asked Congress for another $83.4 billion for the wars in Afghanistan and Iraq. That funding was then increased to $94.2 billion by the House Appropriations Committee, and is about to go before Congress for a vote. Members of Congress need to hear from as many of their constituents as possible that this war funding bill is unacceptable! Please call your Congress person today and tell them to oppose the bill. There is no no military solution to the problems of Iraq, Afghanistan or Pakistan. The American air strikes inside Afghanistan and Pakistan are stirring up more suffering, fear and hatred towards the United States, while decreasing the prospects of a negotiated settlement. Congress needs to re-think and re-direct American resources.

EDUCATION:

Are we seeing any real change regarding our education system? JOBS? Please, we need more than military recruitment. POLITICAL PARTIES: The Republicans find themselves cut off from the concrete relationships of neighborhood life. Republicans are so much the party of individualism and freedom these days that they are no longer the party of community and order. This puts them out of touch with the young, who are exceptionally community-oriented. It gives them nothing to say to the lower middle class, who fear that capitalism has gone haywire. It gives them little to say to the upper middle class, who are interested in the environment and other common concerns. They are imprisoned by old themes that no longer resonate. Democrats have been able to establish themselves as the safe and orderly party. President Barack Obama has made responsibility his core theme and has emerged as a calm, reassuring presence (even as he runs up the debt and intervenes rashly in sector after sector).BUT if they are not compliant to the desires of the AMERICAN people, they will soon find that a third party, a real reform party will come on the horison quite fast the next time around. We need third parties more than ever to introduce new ideas into the system, provide an outlet for people unhappy with current government policy, and make it possible for some third party to grow into a new major party, replacing one or both of the existing parties. No one should under-estimate the AMERICAN people. We will remain vigilant; we will take our country back from the foreign & corporate lobbies, and corrupt officials regardless of party. 75% of us are against the idea of GLOBALISM.

U.S. shipped 989 munitions containers to Israel week before Gaza invasion:

In the dying days of the Bush administration, and a week before Israel launched an aerial bombing campaign, followed by a land invasion of the Gaza Strip, the U.S. military shipped 989 containers of munitions to Israel. Each container was 20-feet long with a total estimated net weight of 14,000 tons. The shipment reportedly reached Israel last month at

Ashod, 40 kilometers north of Gaza. The huge arsenal of munitions will replenish those expended in the Gaza War. According to Amnesty International in the UK, the shipment included white phosphorous. The international organization says 300 of the containers had been unloaded at Ashod in March by a German cargo ship, Wehr Elb., "We are sure that the consignment contained arms and munitions." We have a strong suspicion that it contained white phosphorous which has been used against civilians in Gaza," Brian Wood, head of Arms Control Campaign at Amnesty International in London said late this week.

"The cargo ship had been chartered and controlled by US Military Sealift Command. It left the USA for Israel on December 20, one week before the start of Israeli attacks on Gaza. The vessel was carrying 989 containers of munitions, each of them 20-feet long with a total estimated net weight of 14,000 tons," he said.

"The world community including the Palestinians should be able to know where the remaining 680 containers on board the Wehr Elbe have gone and why the US is not transparent about the final destination of the dangerous cargo.

"A Pentagon spokesperson confirmed to Amnesty International that "the unloading of the entire US munitions shipment was successfully completed at Ashdod on March 22," Wood pointed out. The spokesperson had said the shipment was destined for a US pre-positioned munitions stockpile in Israel, he said. Under a US-Israel agreement, munitions from this stockpile may be transferred for Israeli use if necessary. "There is a great risk that the new munitions may be used by the Israeli military to commit further violations of international law, like the ones committed during the war in Gaza," Wood said.

"Legally and morally, this US arms shipment should have been halted by the Obama administration given the extent of the evidence showing how military equipment and munitions of this kind were recently used by the Israeli forces for war crimes. Arms supplies in these circumstances are contrary to provisions in US law," he said.

An independent inquiry into possible abuses of international law by both sides in the Gaza conflict has been launched by the United Nations. The panel is being headed by Justice Richard J Goldstone of South Africa. "The victims of this brutal conflict have a right to justice and reparation. The perpetrators on both sides must be held accountable if there is to be an end to the cycles of violence and impunity that have persisted for so long. There must be no excuse for either Israel or the Palestinians not to fully cooperate with the inquiry," Amnesty's Middle East and North Africa Program Director Malcolm Smart said this week.

KABUL, Afghanistan's leading human rights organization said Sunday it was investigating the possibility that white phosphorus was used in a U.S.-Taliban battle that killed scores of Afghans. The U.S. military rejected speculation it had used the weapon but left open the possibility Taliban militants did. White phosphorus was used by Israel in Gaza and rights groups say its use over populated areas can indiscriminately burn civilians and constitutes a war crime. Afghan doctors are concerned over what they are calling "unusual" burns on Afghans wounded in last Monday's battle in Farah province, which President Hamid Karzai has said may have killed 125 to 130 civilians. Allegations that white phosphorus or another chemical may have been used threatens to deepen the controversy over what Afghan officials say could be the worst case of civilian deaths since the 2001 U.S. invasion that ousted the Taliban regime. The incident in Farah drew the condemnation of Karzai who called for an end to air strikes.

Nader Nadery, a commissioner for the Afghan Independent Human Rights Commission, said officials were concerned white phosphorus may have been used, but he said more investigation was needed. "Our teams have met with patients," Nadery told The Associated Press. "They are investigating the cause of the injuries and the use of white phosphorus." White phosphorus is a spontaneously flammable material that can cause painful chemical burns. It is used to mark targets, create smoke screens or as a weapon, and can be delivered by shells, flares or hand grenades, according to GlobalSecurity.org.

Human rights groups denounce its use for the severe burns it causes, though it is not banned by any treaty to which the United States is a signatory. The U.S. military used white phosphorus in the battle of Fallujah in Iraq in November 2004. Israel's military used it in January against Hamas targets in Gaza.

Col. Greg Julian, the top U.S. military spokesman in Afghanistan, said the U.S. did not use white phosphorus as a weapon in last week's battle. The U.S. does use white phosphorous to illuminate the night sky, he said. Julian noted that military officials believe that Taliban militants have used white phosphorus at least four times in Afghanistan in the past two years. "I don't know if they (militants) had it out there or not, but it's not out of the question," he said. A spokesman for the Taliban could not be reached for comment Sunday.

The U.S. military on Saturday said that Afghan doctors in Farah told American officials that the injuries seen in wounded Afghans from two villages in the province's Bala Baluk district could have resulted from hand grenades or exploding propane tanks.

Dr. Mohammad Aref Jalali, the head of the burn unit at the Herat Regional Hospital in western Afghanistan who has treated five patients wounded in the battle, described the burns as "unusual."

"I think it's the result of a chemical used in a bomb, but I'm not sure what kind of chemical. But if it was a result of a burning house from petrol or gas cylinders that kind of burn would look different," he said. Gul Ahmad Ayubi, the deputy head of Farah's health department, said the province's main hospital had received 14 patients after the battle, all with burn wounds.

"There have been other air strikes in Farah in the past. We had injuries from those battles, but this is the first time we have seen such burns on the bodies. I'm not sure what kind of bomb it was," he said. U.N. human rights investigators have also seen "extensive" burn wounds on victims and have raised questions about how the injuries were caused, said a U.N. official who asked not to be identified talking about internal

deliberations. The U.N. has reached no conclusions about whether any chemical weapons may have been used,
the official said.

Afghan officials say up to 147 people may have died in the battle in Farah, though the U.S. says that number is exaggerated. The U.S. on Saturday blamed Taliban militants for causing the deaths by using villagers as human shields in the hopes they would be killed. A preliminary U.S. report did not say how many people died in the battle. The investigation into the Farah battle coincides with an appeal by Human Rights Watch for NATO forces to release results of an investigation into a March 14 incident in which an 8-year-old Afghan girl was burned by white phosphorus munitions in Kapisa province.
The New York-based group said Saturday white phosphorus "causes horrendous burns and should not be used in civilian areas."

How many police does it take to silence the voice of the people?

That's a question a despot might ask in a totalitarian police state. But this week the Senate Finance Committee thought it was a hilarious joke as they ejected one brave activist after another, for protesting that not even one spokesperson for single payer health care was being allowed to sit at the hearing table. Yes, Senator Max Baucus (MT), who had preemptively declared that consideration of a single payer option was off the table, actually joked "We need more police [1:58 on video]." And the rest of the Senate panel just laughed their heads off.

Senator Chuck Grassley (IA), the ranking Republican, not to be outdone in his contempt for the people, then asked if there was "Somewhere they can watch it on television [2:05 on video]," which elicited additional hearty guffaws. Yes, what a wonderful entertaining show that would be, the spectacle of the will of the people being excluded while corporate special interests, like butchers, carve up our pocketbooks and our bodies.

On the action page is an extended video where you can hear for yourself those Senators laughing at us, and you'll be just at outraged as we are. It's time for the U.S. Senate to get the message that we the people are not just a joke to be laughed off. Why is it that not ONE senator on that committee has the integrity to stand up for a even handed debate of health care issues? Why should any of them be elected to public office ever again?

So let's see a show of hands. How many of you would like to sign up now for a commie Marxist national health care system like in Canada, England and other pinko Bolshevik countries like that? How stupid do they think we are, to try to reduce the terms of the debate to such an ignorant level? Meet the new mass media scare label, socialized" medicine. As opposed to like what the ANTI-social corporate medical insurance industry we have now, where patients have no role except to be cash cows, by design never to be actually cured? If you or anyone in your family has ever been seriously ill, and as we ALL will be someday, you know the medical industry will pick your bones clean of every dime you ever earned in your life, just in time to drop you into the cheapest possible pine box.

Why are members of Congress fighting so hard to keep single payer health care out of the public debate? Because there are no fat profits in it for their special interest corporate campaign contributors, who maximize their profits the sicker we are. They cannot compete with a low overhead efficiently run government program, just like we have NOW with the existing proven Medicare system.

Instead, they will line up a bunch of corporate lobbyists and stooges to tell bald faced lies. Just like Senator Jim Bunning himself who asserted that Canada and England had tax rate of at LEAST 60% to support single payer. But they don't even want anyone around to even have a chance to call them out on their willful and malicious lies.
Yes, all those who love to preach to the rest of us about the free market and competition are shown to be only interested in a rigged market and a rigged debate. Baucus may put on a face of being slightly chastened, but he STILL will not allow any honest testimony on single payer. But we can beat them.

This is the pivotal moment. We have been speaking out for HR 676 (Medicare for all), for YEARS. And now 8 incredibly brave activists have been hauled away because they would not remain silent. But in doing so, in putting their own bodies on the line, they have shown up the current "debate" for the total sham that it is.

We are not asking you to put your body on the line. All we are asking you to do is submit a one click action page that we have specially configured to send your message to the Senate Finance Committee as a hard copy pdf that they can't just laugh off, because it will be part of the permanent record. Plus your message will go to all your regular members of Congress, plus your nearest daily local newspaper as well if that option is selected. At 3:20 of the video posted on the action page above you will hear a woman loudly ask, "I wonder how many there are?" Let's show them. Let's show them there are millions and millions us out here who will no longer be ignored, who will no longer be laughed off. Because they KNOW we can stop them if and only if large numbers of us will raise our voices now. Let's just do it. And here is a list of all Senators on the Finance Committee, including at least a couple who you might have considered to be
"liberals". Where are their voices? Is there not a single one of them who will stand
up and say, "No wait a minute, we need to hear what the single payer advocates have to say." So especially if one of these is one of YOUR personal Senator, they especially need to hear from you now.

Max BAUCUS, MT, John D. ROCKEFELLER IV, WV, Kent CONRAD, ND, Jeff
BINGAMAN, NM, John F. KERRY, MA, Blanc L. LINCOLN, AR, Ron WYDEN,
OR, Charles E. SCHUMER, NY, Debbie STABENOW, MI, Maria CANTWELL, WA,
Bill NELSON, FL, Robert MENENDEZ, NJ, Thomas CARPER, DE, Chuck
GRASSLEY, IA, Orrin G. HATCH, UT, Olympia J. SNOWE, ME, Jon KYL, AZ,

Jim BUNNING, KY, Mike CRAPO, ID, Pat ROBERTS, KS, John ENSIGN, NV,
Mike ENZI, WY, John CORNYN, TX,

No, we don't need more police. We need fewer Senators with plugs in their ears like Max Baucus. And he and the rest of them need to hear that. And yes, you can also respond to this action through the new Twitter gateway. Just send the following Twitter reply, and add any personal comment you like.

Please take action NOW, so we can win all victories that are supposed to be ours, and forward this alert as widely as possible. Mazin Qumsiyeh is a tireless activist for Palestinian human rights who returned to his hometown of Beit Sahour in the Israeli-occupied West Bank last year and now teaches at Bethlehem and Birzeit Universities. The author of Sharing the Land of Canaan: Human Rights and the Israeli-Palestinian Struggle (2004), Qumsiyeh is both a human rights activist and a scientist who has a lengthy list of publications on genetics to his credit. The Electronic Intifada contributor Ida Audeh met with him in April and discussed advocating the Palestinian cause in the United States and his impressions about the current direction of the Palestinian struggle.

During the 29 years he lived in the United States, Qumsiyeh earned masters and doctoral degrees; taught at several prestigious universities, including Duke and Yale; co-founded activist organizations (Al-Awda, the Palestinian Right to Return Coalition and the Wheels of Justice Tour -- a traveling tour bus that stops at different communities to educate them about Palestine and Iraq); and was a board member for numerous organizations. Since the mid-1990s, he has maintained email lists that focus on human rights and international law. His weekly postings now reach approximately 50,000 individuals and include reports of events and comments that are informed by a deep understanding of common struggles in other parts of the world. An optimist who advocates "having joyful participation in the sorrows of this world," he includes in every e-mail at least one action that the reader can take to make a difference.

Ida Audeh: How would you describe the evolution of perceptions of the Palestinian question and advocacy efforts over the 29 years in which you lived in the United States?

Mazin Qumsiyeh: When I went to the US in August 1979, my impression was that the Zionist narrative was dominant in the churches, the synagogues, the media, community centers, everywhere. There were only a few heroic voices of opposition -- people like Edward Said, Naseer Aruri and Elaine Hagopian -- who influenced me a lot in those early years. They really envisioned changing perceptions by speaking about human rights and international law and actual facts on the ground. Things have changed significantly over the years as more people became informed and educated. Nonprofit organizations have been set up and people are doing good work, including meeting with their congressional representatives.

IA: There has been undeniable progress, but are we doing what needs to be done?

MQ: The question I would ask is, are we doing enough? Of course not. Are we doing well? I think we are doing fairly well. We are moving in the right direction, I'd say that that's probably more relevant than anything else. It is not easy. We are faced with an enemy that is very well organized, well financed, and well entrenched into the system of Western government, as we saw most recently in the Durban Review Conference in Geneva, where the representatives of the US, Canada, Australia and white European countries walked out of the conference hall when Iranian President Mahmoud Ahmadinejad spoke. Those are the countries where the work needs to be done. The question for me is what can I do, and where do I fit as an individual. I don't want to change the world; I just want to push in the direction of justice and human rights.

IA: Dealing with Zionist opposition is straightforward in some ways, because one knows what to expect. But liberals argue the "need" to establish good faith by engaging in dialogue with those whose political values in many instances are hostile to our own.

MQ: Within the so-called liberal peace-oriented movement, there are lots of Zionists with a tribalistic form of nationalism that they hide very well. They claim that they are for peace and for justice and a two-state solution, but when you scratch the surface a little bit, you find that they are racist. One simple test to ask is about the right of return for Palestinian refugees. That immediately exposes what they really think.

That's one aspect. The other aspect is best described by Martin Luther King Jr. in his "Letter from a Birmingham Jail," in which he chides white liberals for always counseling patience. Their kind of liberalism is paternalistic and colonialist. It says, "If you just listen to us, if you denounce terrorism and do this or that, then maybe some time in the future, we will have it in our heart to make pressure to ... achieve some justice for the Palestinians." As Martin Luther King Jr. said, I am getting impatient and don't want to waste too much time with that.

IA: In the US, much of the focus of Palestine advocates is on the Israeli occupation of the West Bank and Gaza Strip (referred to by Palestinians as the 1967 occupation). Should we instead emphasize the nature of Israel itself and the racist laws that Palestinian citizens of Israel are subjected to?

MQ: I argue in Sharing the Land of Canaan that the focus on the 1967 occupation is really the wrong focus, because it goes down that slippery slope of justifying what happened before. We should be talking not about occupation but about colonization, which started much earlier than 1967. There is really no difference between what happened before 1967 and after 1967.

IA: I was reading Naomi Klein's The Shock Doctrine, and she describes the Israeli economy as being pretty healthy despite the global recession, in large part because of the number of Israeli companies with a "security" focus.

MQ: Israel is now the biggest exporter of conflicts in the world, in my opinion, surpassing even the United States. For example, the Sri Lankan government uses Israeli weapons and expertise against the Tamils, committing massacres even as we speak. And Israel profits financially. The Israeli economy is booming because it is based on the export of weapons and conflict. In addition, the occupation of the West Bank and Gaza Strip nets Israel billions of dollars each year. Approximately 40 to 45 percent of all humanitarian aid into the Occupied Palestinian Territory ends up in Israeli hands. This is documented by a series of publications and research on the economy of the occupation by Israeli researcher Sher Hever of the Alternative Information Center. The occupation is big business.

IA: Since 2003 I've visited Palestinian towns and villages in the path of the wall, and someone once told me that each village has its own personal tragedy. How would you describe Bethlehem's tragedy?

MQ: The West Bank has Israeli-imposed colonial settlement infrastructure like roads, sewage systems and electric grids. This is built on top of an existing Palestine, an existing group of villages and towns in the West Bank that have been receding into the background over the past 42 years of occupation. The wall makes this literal and concrete, physically removing shrinking Palestinian areas from the landscape and making those that remain into ghettoes and prisons. In the case of Bethlehem, each cluster of villages gets turned into a ghetto with one exit and entrance only to this village or cluster of villages. There are more than 30 such cantons now in the West Bank. In the Bethlehem area, for example, the villages of Nahalin Bettir, Wadi Fukin and other places that are close to the green line [the 1949 armistice line marking the boundary between Israel and the West Bank] are isolated and surrounded by settlements. The Bethlehem district, which includes Beit Sahour and Beit Jala, is surrounded by walls and settlements from the north, the west and the south. There is an area to the east, called Ush Ghrab, that the settlers would like to take over. If they succeed, there will be settlements on all four sides. Right now the Bethlehem district has only one entrance and exit going to the north of the West Bank and another going south to Hebron. So if those access points are shut off, people won't be able to move anywhere.

IA: Many argue that the Palestinian Authority (PA) functions as a subcontractor for the Israeli occupation. Do you see any positive role that the PA can play? Should we be taking to the streets and demanding its resignation?

MQ: [The late Palestinian thinker] Edward Said described the Oslo process [of the mid-1990s] as the worst thing that happened to the Palestinians since the beginning of the Nakba. The Oslo process put in place this slippery slope of endless negotiations while Israel creates facts on the ground and legitimizes Israel's racist structure, institutions, mechanisms and racist demands for its own security at the expense of Palestinians' basic human rights. Even Amnesty International attributed the failure of Oslo to the fact that it ignored human rights. In any case, Oslo is finished. It was supposed to last for five years, from 1993 to 1999. It expired 10 years ago. We need to reevaluate what happened.

Whether we really need a PA or not is another issue. I for one would prefer no PA, because you cannot have one under occupation. It's a misnomer. What we have is more like prisoners being allowed to elect their prison representatives in negotiations with the jailers. One accommodating side is like the village leagues [of the 1970s] in some sense. Other prisoners elect tougher reps to the authorities. In my opinion, dismantle the Palestinian Authority and say to the international community, we are done with this process that started in Oslo. What you need to do is implement international law and take responsibility for boycotting, divesting from and sanctioning Israel until it complies with international law and basic human rights. After Israel complies, we can create our own institutions, which can then negotiate with Israel.

IA: After the dispossession of historic Palestine in 1948, many Palestinians were dependent on handouts from UNRWA, the UN agency for Palestine refugees, and today tens of thousands are dependent on foreign aid through PA salaries. How do we overcome this situation, which puts us at the mercy of foreign donors and their agendas?

MQ: It is inevitable that people will experience pain if they want their freedom. Although tens of thousands of families depend on salaries from the PA, they still remain a minority of the Palestinian population. The majority of the population is not receiving any salaries, and those people should rise up, and even those who do receive salaries will tell you that they are willing to sacrifice if others do.

[As for the matter of us turning against each other to secure the flow of aid,] that's where leadership is important. If we had decent leadership, they could go to Arab and other countries that want to support us and say that we want to establish mechanisms whereby our people are independent of this. I am sure they could have done it. But it requires leadership instead of these spineless negotiations that end up perpetuating a cycle of colonization and impoverishment and dependency, which reinforces the occupation and colonization.

IA: Do you see any role for the Palestinian political factions?

MQ: We don't have much choice. Fateh and Hamas have large popular backing, and we have to work with all existing factions. We need to educate them; we need to encourage them to adopt changes.

IA: Can you comment on the one-state solution versus two-state solution debate?

MQ: People have to understand the implications and ramifications of support for two states and for one state. We should start with the premise that human rights are inalienable, that there is no compromise on human rights. This means that supporting a two-state solution does not entitle you to oppose the right of return. To do so would be an unacceptable selling out of human rights based on political considerations. If you support two states and also support the right of return, then that's fine by me. Studies by Salman Abu Sitta and others show that most of the villages from which Palestinians were expelled are still empty; people could return to them.

On every level, ranging from the environment, to population growth, to natural resources like water, to theology and ideology -- on every issue that you look at, the possibility and the probability and the desirability of the one-state option far surpasses that of the two-state solution. People frequently cite the two-state option as more achievable, when in fact the likelihood of a truly sovereign Palestinian state in the West Bank and Gaza is infinitesimally smaller than the possibility of a one-state solution. When you talk about two states, are you talking about two sovereign states, with equal rights and responsibilities? Or is it a Bantustan called Palestine and a Jewish state that is nuclear, armed to the teeth, and controls natural resources, air space and so on? If it is the latter, which is what most Israelis seem to support, then that is not a viable solution. If it is the former, most Israelis do not support it and will never support it. If I were in their shoes, I am not sure I would support it; I would support one state because it would enhance my security and be better in every way.

IA: Official discourse on the two-state option makes reference to a territorial swap, which means Israel relinquishing the Palestinian-populated Galilee area in exchange for the settlement blocs in the West Bank. What would that entail?

MQ: This is part of the reason why a two-state option cannot be successful. The Palestinian vision of two states consists of sovereign Israeli and Palestinian states. But for Israeli supporters of a two-state option, there would be something called a Jewish state, which is based on Jewish supremacist ideology and a Jewish majority running state affairs and a minority that (if it is allowed to remain) would be subservient and would be discriminated against. The Palestinian state would also be subservient as a state to the Jewish state and would have no control over its borders or its air space or its natural resources. From a Palestinian and human rights perspective, this is not acceptable.

IA: Is Palestinian society sufficiently mobilized to prevent a sellout of our rights from happening?

MQ: History offers no guarantees. Our situation could turn out like that of the Native Americans, where the probability of them reclaiming their ancestral lands is minimal to zero. Or there is Algeria, where fourth- or fifth-generation French settlers had to pack up and go back to Europe after one million Algerians lost their lives in the struggle for freedom and liberation from the French. In South Africa, the whites were integrated into society, and one person, one vote became a one-state solution. ... I prefer the South African model because it opens the possibility for coexistence and a more durable peace. It is not based on total subjugation of the natives or on total removal of the colonial settlers. The South African model is not ideal, there is still economic apartheid, but at least it eliminated political apartheid and it opens the possibility for a struggle for economic justice and the opportunity to achieve economic justice without violence. ... Although I cannot predict the future, I am optimistic, I think we are moving in the right direction despite the obstacles and despite the physical and metaphysical walls.

IA: Why are you optimistic?

MQ: The Zionist project started out in the middle of the 19th century with support from Britain, and the first Zionist colony in Palestine was established in [1878]. The original Zionist plan included establishing a Jewish empire in the Middle East from the Nile to the Euphrates. That was the goal of most Zionists who advocated a political Zionist project in Palestine. And now, almost 130 years later, that project has failed to achieve a fraction of that goal. From the River Jordan to the Mediterranean, there are 5 million Palestinians. When the Zionist project started in 1880, there were maybe less than 500,000 or 600,000 Palestinians living here. So there is natural increase. And then there are another 5 million Palestinians outside Palestine, and they are doing great work. [Israel's first prime minister, David] Ben Gurion's statement that the old would die and the young would forget has been proven at least half wrong. The old do die, but the young never forget. That's why I believe that there is cause for optimism.

Every day in Palestine, I witness hundreds of instances of brilliant actions. [Besides] the usual forms of resistance, even breathing the air here, having a married life or going to school are all forms of resistance, because we are not wanted in our own land. I find that ingenuity in resistance, the ability to persevere -- what we call sumud -- to be tremendously inspiring. Our people are able to continue their lives despite the incredible odds arrayed against them and not only to persist but also to find some measure of success. As the graffiti on the wall says, to exist is to resist.

PRESSURE OF EXPANDED WAR:

Yes, Stanley McChrystal is the general from the dark side (and proud of it). So the recent sacking of Afghan commander General David McKiernan after less than a year in the field and McChrystal's appointment as the man to run the Afghan War seems to signal that the Obama administration is going for broke. It's heading straight into what, in the Vietnam era, was known as "the big muddy."

General McChrystal comes from a world where killing by any means is the norm and a blanket of secrecy provides the necessary protection. For five years he commanded the Pentagon's super-secret Joint Special Operations Command (JSOC), which, among other things, ran what Seymour Hersh has described as an"executive assassination wing" out of Vice President Cheney's office. (Cheney just returned the favor by givingthe newly appointed general a ringing endorsement: "I think you'd be hard put to find anyone better than Stan McChrystal.")

McChrystal gained a certain renown when President Bush outed him as the man responsible for tracking down and eliminating al-Qaeda-in-Mesopotamia leader Abu Musab al-Zarqawi. The secret force of "manhunters" he commanded had its own secret detention and interrogation center near Baghdad, Camp Nama, where bad things happened regularly, and the unit there, Task Force 6-26, had its own slogan: "If you don't make them bleed, they can't prosecute for it." Since some of the task force's men were, in the end, prosecuted, the bleeding evidently wasn't avoided.

In the Bush years, McChrystal was reputedly extremely close to Secretary of Defense Donald Rumsfeld. The super-secret force he commanded was, in fact, part of Rumsfeld's effort to seize control of, and Pentagonize, the covert, on-the-ground activities that were once the purview of the CIA.

Behind McChrystal lies a string of targeted executions that may run into the hundreds, as well as accusations of torture and abuse by troops under his command (and a role in the cover-up of the circumstances surrounding the death of Army Ranger and former National Football League player Pat Tillman). The general has reportedly long thought of Afghanistan and Pakistan as a single battlefield, which means that he was a premature adherent to the idea of an Af-Pak -- that is, expanded -- war. While in Afghanistan in 2008, the New York Times reported, he was a "key advocate... of a plan, ultimately approved by President George W. Bush, to use American commandos to strike at Taliban sanctuaries in Pakistan." This end-of-term Bush program provoked such anger and blowback in Pakistan that it was reportedly halted after two cross-border raids, one of which killed civilians.

All of this offers more than a hint of the sort of "new thinking and new approaches" -- to use Secretary of Defense Robert Gates's words -- that the Obama administration expects General McChrystal to bring to the devolving Af-Pak battlefield. He is, in a sense, both a legacy figure from the worst days of the Bush-Cheney-Rumsfeld era and the first-born child of Obama-era Washington's growing desperation and hysteria over the wars it inherited.

We loved him back in 2006, when Bush first outed him and Newsweek reporters Michael Hirsh and John Barry dubbed him "a rising star" in the Army and one of the "Jedi Knights who are fighting in what Cheney calls 'the shadows.'"

It's no different today in what's left of the mainstream news analysis business. In that mix of sports lingo, Hollywood-ese, and just plain hyperbole that makes armchair war strategizing just so darn much fun, Washington Post columnist David Ignatius, for instance, claimed that Centcom commander General David Petraeus, who picked McChrystal as his man in Afghanistan, is "assembling an all-star team" and that McChrystal himself is "a rising superstar who, like Petraeus, has helped reinvent the U.S. Army." Is that all?

When it came to pure, instant hagiography, however, the prize went to Elisabeth Bumiller and Mark Mazzetti of the New York Times, who wrote a front-pager, "A General Steps from the Shadows," that painted a picture of McChrystal as a mutant cross between Superman and a saint.

Among other things, it described the general as "an ascetic who... usually eats just one meal a day, in the evening, to avoid sluggishness. He is known for operating on a few hours' sleep and for running to and from work while listening to audio books on an iPod... [He has] an encyclopedic, even obsessive, knowledge about the lives of terrorists... [He is] a warrior-scholar, comfortable with diplomats, politicians..." and so on. The quotes Bumiller and Mazzetti dug up from others were no less spectacular: "He's got all the Special Ops attributes, plus an intellect." "If you asked me the first thing that comes to mind about General McChrystal... I think of no body fat."

From the gush of good cheer about his appointment, you might almost conclude that the general was not human at all, but an advanced android (a good one, of course!) and the "elite" world (of murder and abuse) he emerged from an unbearably sexy one.

Above all, as we're told here and elsewhere, what's so good about the new appointment is that General McChrystal is "more aggressive" than his stick-in-the-mud predecessor. He will, as Bumiller and Thom Shanker report in another piece, bring "a more aggressive and innovative approach to a worsening seven-year war." The general, we're assured, likes operations without body fat, but with plenty of punch. And though no one quite says this, given his closeness to Rumsfeld and possibly Cheney, both desperately eager to "take the gloves off" on a planetary scale, his mentality is undoubtedly a global-war-on-terror one, which translates into no respect for boundaries, restraints, or the sovereignty of others. After all, as journalist Gareth Porter pointed out recently in a thoughtful Asia Times portrait of the new Afghan War commander, Secretary of Defense Donald Rumsfeld granted the parent of JSOC, the Special Operations Command (SOCOM), "the authority to carry out actions unilaterally anywhere on the globe."

Think of McChrystal's appointment, then, as a decision in Washington to dispatch the bull directly to the China shop with the most meager of hopes that the results won't be smashed Afghans and Pakistanis. The Post'sIgnatius even compares McChrystal's boss Petraeus and Obama's special envoy to the region, Richard Holbrooke, to "two headstrong bulls in a small paddock." He then concludes his paean to all of them with this passage -- far more ominous than he means it to be:

"Obama knows the immense difficulty of trying to fix a broken Afghanistan and make it a functioning, modern country. But with his two bulls, Petraeus and Holbrooke, he's marching his presidency into the 'graveyard of empires' anyway."

McChrystal is evidently the third bull, the one slated to start knocking over the tombstones.

An Expanding Af-Pak War

Of course, there are now so many bulls in this particular China shop that smashing is increasingly the name of the game. At this point, the early moves of the Obama administration, when combined with the momentum of the situation it inherited, have resulted in the expansion of the Af-Pak War in at least six areas, which only presage further expansion in the months to come:

1. Expanding Troop Commitment: In February, President Obama ordered a "surge" of 17,000 extra troops into Afghanistan, increasing U.S. forces there by 50%. (Then-commander McKiernan had called for 30,000 new troops.) In March, another 4,000 American military advisors and trainers were promised. The first of the surge troops, reportedly ill-equipped, are already arriving. In March, it was announced that this troop surge would be accompanied by a "civilian surge" of diplomats, advisors, and the like; in April, it was reported that, because the requisite diplomats and advisors couldn't be found, the civilian surge would actually be made up largely of military personnel.

In preparation for this influx, there has been massive base and outpost building in the southern parts of that country, including the construction of 443-acre Camp Leatherneck in that region's "desert of death." When finished, it will support up to 8,000 U.S. troops, and a raft of helicopters and planes. Its airfield, which is under construction, has been described as the "largest such project in the world in a combat setting."

2. Expanding CIA Drone War: The CIA is running an escalating secret drone war in the skies over the Pakistani borderlands with Afghanistan, a "targeted" assassination program of the sort that McChrystal specialized in while in Iraq. Since last September, more than three dozen drone attacks -- the Los Angeles Times put the number at 55 -- have been launched, as opposed to 10 in 2006-2007. The program has reportedly taken out a number of mid-level al-Qaeda and Taliban leaders, but also caused significant civilian casualties, destabilized the Pashtun border areas of Pakistan, and fostered support for the Islamic guerrillas in those regions. As Noah Shachtman wrote recently at his Danger Room website:

"According to the American press, a pair of missiles from the unmanned aircraft killed 'at least 25 militants.' In the local media, the dead were simply described as '29 tribesmen present there.' That simple difference in description underlies a serious problem in the campaign against the Taliban and Al Qaeda. To Americans, the drones over Pakistan are terrorist-killers. In Pakistan, the robotic planes are wiping out neighbors."

David Kilcullen, a key advisor to Petraeus during the Iraq "surge" months, and counterinsurgency expert Andrew McDonald Exum recently called for a moratorium on these attacks on the New York Times op-ed page. ("Press reports suggest that over the last three years drone strikes have killed about 14 terrorist leaders. But, according to Pakistani sources, they have also killed some 700 civilians. This is 50 civilians for every militant killed, a hit rate of 2 percent -- hardly 'precision.'") As it happens, however, the Obama administration is deeply committed to its drone war. As CIA Director Leon Panetta put the matter, "Very frankly, it's the only game in town in terms of confronting or trying to disrupt the al Qaeda leadership."

3. Expanding Air Force Drone War: The U.S. Air Force now seems to be getting into the act as well. There areconflicting reports about just what it is trying to do, but it has evidently brought its own set of Predator and Reaper drones into play in Pakistani skies, in conjunction, it seems, with a somewhat reluctant Pakistani military. Though the outlines of this program are foggy at best, this nonetheless represents an expansion of the war.

4. Expanding Political Interference: Quite a different kind of escalation is also underway. Washington is evidently attempting to insert yet another figure from the Bush-Cheney-Rumsfeld era into the Afghan mix. Not so long ago, Zalmay Khalilzad, the neocon former American viceroy in Kabul and then Baghdad, was considering making a run for the Afghan presidency against Hamid Karzai, the leader the Obama administration is desperate to ditch. In March, reports -- hotly denied by Holbrooke and others -- broke in theBritish press of a U.S./British plan to "undermine President Karzai of Afghanistan by forcing him to install a powerful chief of staff to run the Government." Karzai, so the rumors went, would be reduced to "figurehead" status, while a "chief executive with prime ministerial-style powers" not provided for in the Afghan Constitution would essentially take over the running of the weak and corrupt government.

This week, Helene Cooper reported on the front page of the New York Times that Khalilzad would be that man. He "could assume a powerful, unelected position inside the Afghan government under a plan he is discussing with Hamid Karzai, the Afghan president, according to senior American and Afghan officials." He would then be "the chief executive officer of Afghanistan."

Cooper's report is filled with official denials that these negotiations involve Washington in any way. Yet if they succeed, an American citizen, a former U.S. Ambassador to the U.N. as well as to Kabul, would end up functionally atop the Karzai government just as the

Obama administration is eagerly pursuing a stepped-up war against the Taliban.

Why officials in Washington imagine that Afghans might actually accept such a figure is the mystery of the moment. It's best to think of this plan as the kinder, gentler, soft-power version of the Kennedy administration's 1963 decision to sign off on the coup that led to the assassination of South Vietnamese autocrat Ngo Dinh Diem. Then, too, top Washington officials were distressed that a puppet who seemed to be losing support was, like Karzai, also acting in an increasingly independent manner when it came to playing his appointed role in an American drama. That assassination, by the way, only increased instability in South Vietnam, leading to a succession of weak military regimes and paving the way for a further unraveling there. This American expansion of the war would likely have similar consequences.

5. Expanding War in Pakistan: Meanwhile, in Pakistan itself, mayhem has ensued, again in significant part thanks to Washington, whose disastrous Afghan war and escalating drone attacks have helped to destabilize the Pashtun regions of the country. Now, the Pakistani military -- pushed and threatened by Washington (with the loss of military aid, among other things) -- has smashed full force into the districts of Buner and Swat, which had, in recent months, been largely taken over by the Islamic fundamentalist guerrillas we call "the Pakistani Taliban."

It's been a massive show of force by a military configured for smash-mouth war with India, not urban or village warfare with lightly armed guerrillas. The Pakistani military has loosed its jets, helicopter gunships, and artillery on the region (even as the CIA drone strikes continue), killing unknown numbers of civilians and, far more significantly, causing a massive exodus of the local population. In some areas, well more than half the population has fled Taliban depredations and indiscriminate fire from the military. Those that remain in besieged towns and cities, often without electricity, with the dead in the streets, and fast disappearing supplies of food, are clearly in trouble.

With nearly 1.5 million Pakistanis turned into refugees just since the latest offensive began, U.N. officials are suggesting that this could be the worst refugee crisis since the Rwandan genocide in 1994. Talk about the destabilization of a country.

In the long run, this may only increase the anger of Pashtuns in the tribal areas of Pakistan at both the Americans and the Pakistani military and government. The rise of Pashtun nationalism and a fight for an"Islamic Pashtunistan" would prove a dangerous development indeed. This latest offensive is what Washington thought it wanted, but undoubtedly the old saw, "Be careful what you wish for, lest it come true," applies. Already a panicky Washington is planning to rush $110 million in refugee assistance to the country.

6. Expanding Civilian Death Toll and Blowback: As Taliban attacks in Afghanistan rise and that loose guerrilla force (more like a coalition of various Islamist, tribal, warlord, and criminal groups) spreads into new areas, the American air war in Afghanistan continues to take a heavy toll on Afghan civilians, while manufacturing ever more enemies as well as deep resentment and protest in that country. The latest such incident, possibly the worst since the Taliban was defeated in 2001, involves the deaths of up to 147 Afghans in the Bala Baluk district of Farah Province, according to accounts that have come out of the villages attacked. Up to 95 of the dead were under 18, one Afghan lawmaker involved in investigating the incident claims, and up to 65 of them women or girls. These deaths came after Americans were called into an escalating fight between the Taliban and Afghan police and military units, and in turn, called in devastating air strikes by two U.S. jets and a B-1 bomber (which, villagers claim, hit them after the Taliban fighters had left).

Despite American pledges to own up to and apologize more quickly for civilian deaths, the post-carnage events followed a predictable stonewalling pattern, including a begrudging step-by-step retreat in the face of independent claims and reports. The Americans first denied that anything much had happened; then claimed that they had killed mainly Taliban "militants"; then that the Taliban had themselves used grenades to kill most of the civilians (a charge later partially withdrawn as "thinly sourced"); and finally, that the numbers of Afghan dead were "extremely over-exaggerated," and that the urge for payment from the Afghan government might be partially responsible.

An investigation, as always, was launched that never seems to end, while the Americans wait for the story to fade from view. As of this moment, while still awaiting the results of a "very exhaustive" investigation, American spokesmen nonetheless claim that only 20-30 civilians died along with up to 65 Taliban insurgents. In these years, however, the record tells us that, when weighing the stories offered by surviving villagers and those of American officials, believe the villagers. Put more bluntly, in such situations, we lie, they die.

Two things make this "incident" at Bala Baluk more striking. First of all, according to Jerome Starkey of the British Independent, another Rumsfeld creation, the U.S. Marines Corps Special Operations Command (MarSOC), the Marines' version of JSOC, was centrally involved, as it had been in two other major civilian slaughters, one near Jalalabad in 2007 (committed by a MarSOC unit that dubbed itself "Taskforce Violence"), the second in 2008 at the village of Azizabad in Herat Province. McChrystal's appointment, reports Starkey, has "prompted speculation that [similar] commando counterinsurgency missions will increase in the battle to beat the Taliban."

Second, back in Washington, National Security Advisor James Jones and head of the Joint Chiefs Admiral Mike Mullen, fretting about civilian casualties in Afghanistan and faced with President Karzai's repeated pleas to cease air attacks on Afghan villages, nonetheless refused to consider the possibility. Both, in fact, used the same image. As Jones told ABC's George Stephanopoulos: "Well, I think he understands that... we have to have the full complement of... our offensive military power when we need it... We can't fight with one hand tied behind our back..."

In a world in which the U.S. is the military equivalent of the multi-armed Hindu god Shiva, this is one of the truly strange, if long-lasting, American images. It was, for instance, used by President George H. W.

Bush on the eve of the first Gulf War. "No hands," he said, "are going to be tied behind backs. This is not a Vietnam."

Forgetting the levels of firepower loosed in Vietnam, the image itself is abidingly odd. After all, in everyday speech, the challenge "I could beat you with one hand tied behind my back" is a bravado offer of voluntary restraint and an implicit admission that fighting any other way would make one a bully. So hidden in the image, both when the elder Bush used it and today, is a most un-American acceptance of the United States as a bully nation, about to be restrained by no one, least of all itself.

Apologize or stonewall, one thing remains certain: the air war will continue and so civilians will continue to die. The idea that the U.S. might actually be better off with one "hand" tied behind its back is now so alien to us as to be beyond serious consideration.

The Pressure of an Expanding War

President Obama has opted for a down-and-dirty war strategy in search of some at least minimalist form of success. For this, McChrystal is the poster boy. Former Afghan commander General McKiernan believed that, "as a NATO commander, my mandate stops at the [Afghan] border. So unless there is a clear case of self-protection to fire across the border, we don't consider any operations across the border in the tribal areas."

That the "responsibilities" of U.S. generals fighting the Afghan War "ended at the border with Pakistan," Mark Mazzetti and Eric Schmitt of the Times report, is now considered part of an "old mind-set." McChrystal represents those "fresh eyes" that Secretary of Defense Robert Gates talked about in the press conference announcing the general's appointment. As Mazzetti and Schmitt point out, "Among [McChrystal's] last projects as the head of the Joint Special Operations Command was to better coordinate Pentagon and Central Intelligence Agency efforts on both sides of the porous border."

For those old enough to remember, we've been here before. Administrations that start down a path of expansion in such a war find themselves strangely locked in -- psychically, if nothing else -- if things don't work out as expected and the situation continues to deteriorate. In Vietnam, the result was escalation without end. President Obama and his foreign policy team now seem locked into an expanding war. Despite the fact that the application of force has not only failed for years, but actually fed that expansion, they also seem to be locked into a policy of applying ever greater force, with the goal of, as the Post's Ignatius puts it, cracking the "Taliban coalition" and bringing elements of it to the bargaining table.

So keep an eye out for whatever goes wrong, as it most certainly will, and then for the pressures on Washington to respond with further expansions of what is already "Obama's war." With McChrystal in charge in Afghanistan, for instance, it seems reasonable to assume that the urge to sanction new Special Forces raids into Pakistan will grow. After all, frustration in Washington is already building, for however much the Pakistani military may be taking on the Taliban in Swat or Buner, don't expect its military or civilian leaders to be terribly interested in what happens near the Afghan border.

As Tony Karon of the Rootless Cosmopolitan blog puts the matter: "The current military campaign is designed to enforce a limit on the Taliban's reach within Pakistan, confining it to the movement's heartland." And that heartland is the Afghan border region. For one thing, the Pakistani military (and the country's intelligence services, which essentially brought the Taliban into being long ago) are focused on India. They want a Pashtun ally across the border, Taliban or otherwise, where they fear the Indians are making inroads.

So the frustration of a war in which the enemy has no borders and we do is bound to rise along with the fighting, long predicted to intensify this year. We now have a more aggressive "team" in place. Soon enough, if the fighting in the Afghan south and along the Pakistani border doesn't go as planned, pressure for the president to send in those other 10,000 troops General McKiernan asked for may rise as well, as could pressure to apply more air power, more drone power, more of almost anything. And yet, as former CIA station chief in Kabul, Graham Fuller, wrote recently, in the region "crises have only grown worse under the U.S. military footprint." And what if, as the war continues its slow arc of expansion, the "Washington coalition" is the one that cracks first? What then?

Historical amnesia is a dangerous phenomenon, not only because it undermines moral and intellectual integrity, but also because it lays the groundwork for crimes that still lie ahead.

"Racists for Democracy"

HOW LUCKY we are to have the extreme Right standing guard over our democracy.

This week, the Knesset voted by a large majority (47 to 34) for a law that threatens imprisonment for anyone who dares to deny that Israel is a Jewish and Democratic State.

The private member's bill, proposed by MK Zevulun Orlev of the "Jewish Home" party, which sailed through its preliminary hearing, promises one year in prison to anyone who publishes "a call that negates the existence of the State of Israel as a Jewish and Democratic State", if the contents of the call might cause "actions of hate, contempt or disloyalty against the state or the institutions of government or the courts".

One can foresee the next steps. A million and a half Arab citizens cannot be expected to recognize Israel as a Jewish and Democratic State. They want it to be "a state of all its citizens" – Jews, Arabs and others. They also claim with reason that Israel discriminates against them, and therefore is not really democratic. And, in addition, there are also Jews who do not want Israel to be defined as a Jewish State in which non-Jews have the status, at best, of tolerated outsiders.

The consequences are inevitable. The prisons will not be able to hold all those convicted of this crime. There will be a need for concentration camps all over the country to house all the deniers of Israeli democracy. The police will be unable to deal with so many criminals. It will be necessary to set up a new unit. This may be called "Special Security", or, in short, SS.

Hopefully, these measures will suffice to preserve our democracy. If not, more stringent steps will have to be taken, such as revoking the citizenship of the democracy-deniers and deporting them from the country, together with the Jewish leftists and all the other enemies of the Jewish democracy. After the preliminary reading of the bill, it now goes to the Legal Committee of the Knesset, which will prepare it for the first, and soon thereafter for the second and third readings. Within a few weeks or months, it will be the law of the land.

By the way, the bill does not single out Arabs explicitly – even if this is its clear intention, and all those who voted for it understood this. It also prohibits Jews from advocating a change in the state's definition, or the creation of a bi-national state in all of historic Palestine or spreading any other such unconventional ideas. One can only imagine what would happen in the US if a senator proposed a law to imprison anyone who suggests an amendment to the Constitution of the United States of America.

THE BILL does not stand out at all in our new political landscape.:

This government has already adopted a bill to imprison for three years anyone who mourns the Palestinian Naqba – the 1948 uprooting of more than half the Palestinian people from their homes and lands.

The sponsors expect Arab citizens to be happy about that event. True, the Palestinians were caused a certain unpleasantness, but that was only a by-product of the foundation of our state. The Independence Day of the Jewish and Democratic State must fill us all with joy. Anyone who does not express this joy should be locked up, and three years may not be enough.

This bill has been confirmed by the Ministerial Commission for Legal Matters, prior to being submitted to the Knesset. Since the rightist government commands a majority in the Knesset, it will be adopted almost automatically. (In the meantime, a slight delay has been caused by one minister, who appealed the decision, so the Ministerial Commission will have to confirm it again.)

The sponsors of the law hope, perhaps, that on Naqba Day the Arabs will dance in the streets, plant Israeli flags on the ruins of some 600 Arab villages that were wiped off the map and offer up their thanks to Allah in the mosques for the miraculous good fortune that was bestowed on them.

THIS TAKES me back to the 60s, when the weekly magazine I edited, Haolam Hazeh, published an Arabic edition. One of its employees was a young man called Rashed Hussein from the village of Musmus. Already as a youth he was a gifted poet with a promising future.

He told me that some years earlier the military governor of his area had summoned him to his office. At the time, all the Arabs in Israel were subject to a military government which controlled their lives in all matters big and small. Without a permit, an Arab citizen could not leave his village or town even for a few hours, nor get a job as a teacher, nor acquire a tractor or dig a well.

The governor received Rashed cordially, offered him coffee and paid lavish compliments to his poetry. Then he came to the point: in a month's time, Independence Day was due, and the governor was going to hold a big reception for the Arab "notables"; he asked Rashed to write a special poem for the occasion. Rashed was a proud youngster, nationalist to the core, and not lacking in courage. He explained to the governor that Independence Day was no joyful day for him, since his relatives had been driven from their homes and most of the Musmus village's land had also been expropriated. When Rashed arrived back at his village some hours later, he could not help noticing that his neighbors were looking at him in a peculiar way. When he entered his home, he was shocked. All the members of his family were sitting on the floor, the women lamenting at the top of their voices, the children huddling fearfully in a corner. His first thought was that somebody had died.

"What have you done to us!" one of the women cried, "What did we do to you?"

"You have destroyed the family," another shouted, "You have finished us!"

It appeared that the governor had called the family and told them that Rashed had refused to fulfill his duty to the state. The threat was clear: from now on, the extended family, one of the largest in the village, would be on the black list of the military government. The consequences were clear to everyone. Rashed could not stand up against the lamentation of his family. He gave in and wrote the poem, as requested. But something inside him was broken. Some years later he emigrated to the US, got a job there at the PLO office and died tragically: he was burned alive in his bed after going to sleep, it appears, while smoking a cigarette.

THESE DAYS are gone forever. We took part in many stormy demonstrations against the military government until it was finally abolished in 1966. As a newly elected Member of Parliament, I had the privilege of voting for its abolition.

The fearful and subservient Arab minority, then amounting to some 200 thousand souls, has recovered its self-esteem. A second and third generation has grown up, its downtrodden national pride has raised its head again, and today they are a large and self-confident community of 1.5 million. But the attitude of the Jewish Right has not changed for the better. On the contrary.

In the Knesset bakery (the Hebrew word for bakery is Mafia) some new pastries are being baked. One of them is a bill that stipulates that anyone applying for Israeli citizenship must declare their loyalty to "the Jewish, Zionist and Democratic State", and also undertake to serve in the army or its civilian alternative. Its sponsor is MK David Rotem of the "Israel is Our Home" party, who also happens to be the chairman of the Knesset Law Committee.

A declaration of loyalty to the state and its laws – a framework designed to safeguard the wellbeing and the rights of its citizens – is reasonable. But loyalty to the "Zionist" state? Zionism is an ideology, and in a democratic state the ideology can change from time to time. It would be like declaring loyalty to a "capitalist" USA, a "rightist Italy", a "leftist" Spain, a "Catholic Poland" or a "nationalist" Russia.

This would not be a problem for the tens of thousands of Orthodox Jews in Israel who reject Zionism, since Jews will not be touched by this law. They obtain citizenship automatically the moment they arrive in Israel.

Another bill waiting for its turn before the Ministerial Committee proposes changing the declaration that every new Knesset Member has to make before assuming office. Instead of loyalty "to the State of Israel and its laws", as now, he or she will be required to declare their loyalty "to the Jewish, Zionist and Democratic State of Israel, its symbols and its values". That would exclude almost automatically all the elected Arabs, since declaring loyalty to the "Zionist" state would mean that no Arab would ever vote for them again.

It would also be a problem for the Orthodox members of the Knesset, who cannot declare loyalty to Zionism. According to Orthodox doctrine, the Zionists are depraved sinners and the Zionist flag is unclean. God exiled the Jews from this country because of their wickedness, and only God can permit them to return. Zionism, by preempting the job of the Messiah, has committed an unpardonable sin, and many Orthodox Rabbis chose to remain in Europe and be murdered by the Nazis rather than committing the Zionist sin of going to Palestine.

THE FACTORY of racist laws with a distinct fascist odor is now working at full steam. That is built into the new coalition. At its center is the Likud party, a good part of which is pure racist (sorry for the oxymoron). To its right there is the ultra-racist Shas party, to the right of which is Lieberman's ultra-ultra racist "Israel is our Home" party, the ultra-ultra-ultra racist "Jewish Home" party, and to its right the even more racist "National Union" party, which includes outright Kahanists and stands with one foot in the coalition and the other on the moon.

All these factions are trying to outdo each other. When one proposes a crazy bill, the next is compelled to propose an even crazier one, and so on. All this is possible because Israel has no constitution. The ability of the Supreme Court to annul laws that contradict the "basic laws" is not anchored anywhere, and the Rightist parties are trying to abolish it. Not for nothing did Avigdor Lieberman demand – and get – the Justice and Police ministries.

Just now, when the governments of the US and Israel are clearly on a collision course over the settlements, this racist fever may infect all parts of the coalition.

If one goes to sleep with a dog, one should not be surprised to wake up with fleas (may the dogs among my readers pardon me). Those who elected such a government, and even more so those who joined it, should not be surprised by its laws, which ostensibly safeguard Jewish democracy.

The most appropriate name for these holy warriors would be "Racists for Democracy"

HOW LUCKY we are to have the extreme Right standing guard over our democracy.

This week, the Knesset voted by a large majority (47 to 34) for a law that threatens imprisonment for anyone who dares to deny that Israel is a Jewish and Democratic State.

The private member's bill, proposed by MK Zevulun Orlev of the "Jewish Home" party, which sailed through its preliminary hearing, promises one year in prison to anyone who publishes "a call that negates the existence of the State of Israel as a Jewish and Democratic State", if the contents of the call might cause "actions of hate, contempt or disloyalty against the state or the institutions of government or the courts". One can foresee the next steps. A million and a half Arab citizens cannot be expected to recognize Israel as a Jewish and Democratic State. They want it to be "a state of all its citizens" – Jews, Arabs and others. They also claim with reason that Israel discriminates against them, and therefore is not really democratic. And, in addition, there are also Jews who do not want Israel to be defined as a Jewish State in which non-Jews have the status, at best, of tolerated outsiders.

The consequences are inevitable. The prisons will not be able to hold all those convicted of this crime. There will be a need for concentration camps all over the country to house all the deniers of Israeli democracy. The police will be unable to deal with so many criminals. It will be necessary to set up a new unit. This may be called "Special Security", or, in short, SS. Hopefully, these measures will suffice to preserve our democracy. If not, more stringent steps will have to be taken, such as revoking the citizenship of the democracy-deniers and deporting them from the country, together with the Jewish leftists and all the other enemies of the Jewish democracy.

After the preliminary reading of the bill, it now goes to the Legal Committee of the Knesset, which will prepare it for the first, and soon thereafter for the second and third readings. Within a few weeks or months, it will be the law of the land. By the way, the bill does not single out Arabs explicitly – even if this is its clear intention, and all those who voted for it understood this. It also prohibits Jews from advocating a change in the state's definition, or the creation of a bi-national state in all of historic Palestine or spreading any other such unconventional ideas. One can only imagine what would happen in the US if a senator proposed a law to imprison anyone who suggests an amendment to the Constitution of the United States of America.

THE BILL does not stand out at all in our new political landscape.

This government has already adopted a bill to imprison for three years anyone who mourns the Palestinian Naqba – the 1948 uprooting of more than half the Palestinian people from their homes and lands.

The sponsors expect Arab citizens to be happy about that event. True, the Palestinians were caused a certain unpleasantness, but that was only a by-product of the foundation of our state. The Independence Day of the Jewish and Democratic State must fill us all with joy. Anyone who does not express this joy should be locked up, and three years may not be enough.

This bill has been confirmed by the Ministerial Commission for Legal Matters, prior to being submitted to the Knesset. Since the rightist government commands a majority in the Knesset, it will be adopted almost automatically. (In the meantime, a slight delay has been caused by one minister, who appealed the decision, so the Ministerial Commission will have to confirm it again.)

The sponsors of the law hope, perhaps, that on Naqba Day the Arabs will dance in the streets, plant Israeli flags on the ruins of some 600 Arab villages that were wiped off the map and offer up their thanks to Allah in the mosques for the miraculous good fortune that was bestowed on them.

THIS TAKES me back to the 60s, when the weekly magazine I edited, Haolam Hazeh, published an Arabic edition. One of its employees was a young man called Rashed Hussein from the village of Musmus. Already as a youth he was a gifted poet with a promising future.

He told me that some years earlier the military governor of his area had summoned him to his office. At the time, all the Arabs in Israel were subject to a military government which controlled their lives in all matters big and small. Without a permit, an Arab citizen could not leave his village or town even for a few hours, nor get a job as a teacher, nor acquire a tractor or dig a well.

The governor received Rashed cordially, offered him coffee and paid lavish compliments to his poetry. Then he came to the point: in a month's time, Independence Day was due, and the governor was going to hold a big reception for the Arab "notables"; he asked Rashed to write a special poem for the occasion.

Rashed was a proud youngster, nationalist to the core, and not lacking in courage. He explained to the governor that Independence Day was no joyful day for him, since his relatives had been driven from their homes and most of the Musmus village's land had also been expropriated.
When Rashed arrived back at his village some hours later, he could not help noticing that his neighbors were looking at him in a peculiar way.

When he entered his home, he was shocked. All the members of his family were sitting on the floor, the women lamenting at the top of their voices, the children huddling fearfully in a corner. His first thought was that somebody had died.

"What have you done to us!" one of the women cried, "What did we do to you?"

"You have destroyed the family," another shouted, "You have finished us!"

It appeared that the governor had called the family and told them that Rashed had refused to fulfill his duty to the state. The threat was clear: from now on, the extended family, one of the largest in the village, would be on the black list of the military government. The consequences were clear to everyone. Rashed could not stand up against the lamentation of his family. He gave in and wrote the poem, as requested. But something inside him was broken. Some years later he immigrated to the US, got a job there at the PLO office and died tragically: he was burned alive in his bed after going to sleep, it appears, while smoking a cigarette.

THESE DAYS are gone forever. We took part in many stormy demonstrations against the military government until it was finally abolished in 1966. As a newly elected Member of Parliament, I had the privilege of voting for its abolition.

The fearful and subservient Arab minority, then amounting to some 200 thousand souls, has recovered its self-esteem. A second and third generation has grown up, its downtrodden national pride has raised its head again, and today they are a large and self-confident community of 1.5 million. But the attitude of the Jewish Right has not changed for the better. On the contrary.

In the Knesset bakery (the Hebrew word for bakery is Mafia) some new pastries are being baked. One of them is a bill that stipulates that anyone applying for Israeli citizenship must declare their loyalty to "the Jewish, Zionist and Democratic State", and also undertake to serve in the army or its civilian alternative. Its sponsor is MK David Rotem of the "Israel is

Our Home" party, who also happens to be the chairman of the Knesset Law Committee.

A declaration of loyalty to the state and its laws – a framework designed to safeguard the wellbeing and the rights of its citizens – is reasonable. But loyalty to the "Zionist" state? Zionism is an ideology, and in a democratic state the ideology can change from time to time. It would be like declaring loyalty to a "capitalist" USA, a "rightist Italy", a "leftist" Spain, a "Catholic Poland" or a "nationalist" Russia.

This would not be a problem for the tens of thousands of Orthodox Jews in Israel who reject Zionism, since Jews will not be touched by this law. They obtain citizenship automatically the moment they arrive in Israel.

Another bill waiting for its turn before the Ministerial Committee proposes changing the declaration that every new Knesset Member has to make before assuming office. Instead of loyalty "to the State of Israel and its laws", as now, he or she will be required to declare their loyalty "to the Jewish, Zionist and Democratic State of Israel, its symbols and its values". That would exclude almost automatically all the elected Arabs, since declaring loyalty to the "Zionist" state would mean that no Arab would ever vote for them again.

It would also be a problem for the Orthodox members of the Knesset, who cannot declare loyalty to Zionism. According to Orthodox doctrine, the Zionists are depraved sinners and the Zionist flag is unclean. God exiled the Jews from this country because of their wickedness, and only God can permit them to return. Zionism, by preempting the job of the Messiah, has committed an unpardonable sin, and many Orthodox Rabbis chose to remain in Europe and be murdered by the Nazis rather than committing the Zionist sin of going to Palestine.

THE FACTORY of racist laws with a distinct fascist odor is now working at full steam. That is built into the new coalition. At its center is the Likud party, a good part of which is pure racist (sorry for the oxymoron). To its right there is the ultra-racist Shas party, to the right of which is Lieberman's ultra-ultra racist "Israel is our Home" party, the ultra-ultra-ultra racist "Jewish Home" party, and to its right the even more racist "National Union" party, which includes outright Kahanists and stands with one foot in the coalition and the other on the moon.

All these factions are trying to outdo each other. When one proposes a crazy bill, the next is compelled to propose an even crazier one, and so on. All this is possible because Israel has no constitution. The ability of the Supreme Court to annul laws that contradict the "basic laws" is not anchored anywhere, and the Rightist parties are trying to abolish it. Not for nothing did Avigdor Lieberman demand – and get – the Justice and Police ministries.Just now, when the governments of the US and Israel are clearly on a collision course over the settlements, this racist fever may infect all parts of the coalition.

If one goes to sleep with a dog, one should not be surprised to wake up with fleas (may the dogs among my readers pardon me). Those who elected such a government, and even more so those who joined it, should not be surprised by its laws, which ostensibly safeguard Jewish Fascism. The most appropriate name for these holy warriors would be "Racists for Democracy". WATCH-OUT!

MEDIA AND CONGRESSIONAL TREASON:

When Antony Flew became a Deist, he said he did so because he "followed the evidence." This practice and principle of following the evidence wherever it may lead should be employed by everyone and in every aspect of our lives.

When we look at the blind obedience that the overwhelming majority of politicians from both parties give to Israel's lobby group, the American Israel Public Affairs Committee, we need to ask ourselves, why? And we need to follow the evidence we uncover as we pursue an answer.

Aristotle advised, "Let us first understand the facts, and then we may seek the cause." The facts regarding the relationship between AIPAC and the politicians of both parties are: 1. Almost all the politicians regardless of which party they belong to closely follow instructions from AIPAC; 2.

Politicians who show disobedience to AIPAC usually pay a stiff political price; 3. AIPAC has such a grip on the politicians that they routinely put the interests of Israel above the interests of the US; 4. The media rarely if ever reports on these important facts.

Remember when Howard Dean wanted to be the presidential nominee for the Democratic Party? He made the political mistake of saying the US should have a balanced foreign policy for the Middle East. He was instantly attacked by Democrats and Republicans alike! Nancy Pelosi wrote a scathing open letter to Dean stating among other things, "American foreign policy has been -- and must continue to be -- based on unequivocal support for Israel's right to exist and to be free from terror . . . . It is unacceptable for the U.S. to be 'evenhanded' on these fundamental issues . . . ." (As Michael Scheuer points out in his outstanding book Imperial Hubris - Why America is Losing the War on Terror, do Americans really want to put Israel's interests before our own? Are we willing to spend BILLIONS of dollars each and every year and lose the lives of thousands of Americans for Israel?) It wasn't long after Dean's statement calling for an evenhanded US policy in the Middle East that the media ran and continually reran the clip of Dean appearing like a lunatic shouting and yelling during one of his campaign rallies. He was soon out of the race. As Salon.com wrote regarding Dean's situation, ". . . it proves that not showing unequivocal support for the Jewish state remains a political poison pill -- for members of either political party."

The self-serving politicians of both parties get the message loud and clear! In fact, they fight each other as to who favors Israel the most! And it doesn't matter what Israel is doing, the "US" Congress will support the Jewish state! For example, after they invaded Lebanon this past summer, the "US" Senate unanimously passed a resolution blindly supporting the state terrorist acts of Israel against its neighbor while the "US" House of Representatives passed a similar pro-Israel resolution by a vote of 410 to 8! (I'm sure those eight are anti-Semites! LOL!) Since Israel's invasion of Lebanon resulted in the deaths of hundreds of innocent civilians which the Israeli military killed using US weapons given to them by US taxpayers via their elected officials, US weapons such as cluster-bombs that the UN is still trying to clean up, I'm sure we've added a few thousand more Islamic people who are ready to launch attacks against the US to al Qaeda's list of volunteers!

In America we like to pretend we have a "free press" that allows us to get all sides to important issues. Of course, reality is much different! When is the last time you watched a media report on the excessive influence AIPAC has over the plutocrats in Congress and the White House? This has been an important and dangerous reality for the last 20 to 30 years, but I've never seen the media report on it in any meaningful way. With all that is going on now with AIPAC having pushed their kosher politicians to bring America into war in Iraq and with AIPAC and Israel now pushing these same moral cowards for a US war with Iran and Syria, it is of paramount importance that AIPAC and their political whores be thoroughly exposed to the American people.

This silence on the part of the media makes it painfully clear that the media is in the pocket of AIPAC and Israel. Actions, and inactions, speak much louder than words. Perhaps if the media had done their job as a truly free-press over the last few decades and reported to the American people how twisted US policy is in favor of Israel, 9/11 could have been averted.

Another issue that involves the media being biased in favor of Israel is Israel's possession of real Weapons of Mass Destruction. In Seymour Hersh's revealing book about Israel's nuclear arsenal, The Sampson Option, he documents how Israel deceived the US regarding its development and possession of nuclear bombs. Just the other day, Israel's Prime Minister stated, "Can you say that this is the same level when they (Iran) are aspiring to have nuclear weapons, as America, France, Israel, Russia?" He admits that Israel has nukes, yet the American "free press" does virtually nothing! However, the media is very good at confronting Iran in its efforts to acquire nuclear power, which it claims is only for peaceful purposes. Why the double standard? Those masquerading as journalists should be honest with themselves and either write and broadcast what is going on or find other careers.

I've noticed the media toeing the Israeli line regarding the conclusion of the Iraq Study Group that ending the Palestinian subjugation by Israel is key to solving the violence in the Middle East. The Iraq Study Group is not the only ones who realize this. In his book Imperial Hubris, former CIA specialist on Osama bin Laden Michael Scheuer said the same thing. However, Israel doesn't want this fact to be known, and already pro-Israel "journalists" are belittling this important part of the Middle East equation.

One of the reasons former US President Jimmy Carter wrote his interesting and informative book Palestine Peace Not Apartheid was to let people know there is actually another side to the Israeli-Palestinian conflict besides the Jewish side.

When asked why he wrote the book that is being attacked by the media, politicians and Jews, he said it was to give people a different point of view from what they're used to. In other words, the media is not giving us an accurate picture of what is actually going on in Palestine. And the Kosher Iron Curtain we live behind is not allowing us any picture of what is actually going on regarding the blind and ignorant support of Israel that the politicians give in our name.

Two weeks ago, when we learned that the Obama lawyers were going to drop the AIPAC spy case, I was not surprised but also, very disgusted. The clever Zionists working on behalf of a foreign power threatened to uncover ALL of the treason at the top and how complicit our government is, with Israeli spies. We strongly fear that the Mossad/9/11 business would come up and the complicity of our rulers with Zionist aims would be revealed, at last. The wild goose chase after the 'bombs in the buildings' would cease protecting the real traitors and we would be discussing how complicit AIPAC, Mossad and our 'Presidents' really are and how they really operate.

There is no media hysteria about all this, of course. The media giants don't want us to know if they are Zionist dual-citizens working on behalf of a foreign government, for example. The AIPAC trials were barely mentioned in the news and there wasn't a chorus of screaming

Zionists demanding an accounting for this spying. Indeed, the chorus has mostly been screaming about how good torture is for us and how suspending basic Constitutional rights and International laws is OK if it makes us 'safer.'

How on earth can a country be 'safer' if the entire system is riddled with spies, foreign agents, traitorous politicians protecting alien powers which are also looting our Treasury? First, let's go to the EU. The EU has passed many draconian laws forbidding arguments about the Holocaust, Naziism and Zionism. Anyone daring to discuss, even casually, these things, can be summarily arrested and brought before the EU Inquisition.

Similar laws that totally contravene US Constitutional rights are being passed right now, for example. Historians in Europe are muzzled due to fear of being imprisoned if they so much dare to discuss any major issue that is either ethnic or religious in nature. This has shuttered the universities in Europe and is causing a drop in the ability to have an open debate.

I maintain all my life ,that locking things in dark closets simply makes them grow into monsters ,which burst out of these closets. If the Israeli's and their many, many supporters, if the Muslims and their many supporters, want us to think a certain way, they can have an open debate about all things ethnic and religious. I welcome this. But they do NOT want this. Just like the Catholic Church hates open debate about religious matters.

They want to crush secular discussions totally and utterly. This way, the religious powers can lord it over all of us and we have burnings at the stake, persecutions, torture and other features which our Founding Fathers hated so much, they made all this illegal in the Constitution.

Many a brave professor including Finkelstein, the son of victims of Hitler's Holocaust, are given the Spanish Inquisition treatment whenever they dare to mention the obvious connection between the Warsaw Ghetto and the Gaza Ghetto. One problem Jewish Zionists who are bribing Congress to cut our basic freedoms is this: the laws that protect Neo-Nazi Zionism will also protect Muslim radicalism! So long as the Muslims cease attacking the Jews in speeches, etc, but instead, focus on attacking anyone attacking their religious beliefs, this will stop Jews from playing the demonization of Muslims game!

In other words, ultimately, this will backfire. Unless the government and courts establish a two-tier system like the one in Israel where Jews have superior PRIVILEGES compared to others. So they can talk dirty or talk violently while we all have to pussy foot around each other. This can happen and AIPAC will try to make it happen. The joys of their Nazi-state of Israel where Jews can assault other citizens with impunity, talk about annihilating fellow citizens and ejecting them from the country, or other Nazi pastimes, this joy is very addictive. One can parade about openly, strutting and preening just like the Nazis loved strutting. One can demand everyone be very, very careful about talking about say, Jewish ownership of the media, while at the same time, the Jews could discuss any issue they desire, in public, and even be obnoxious and vicious, even issue death threats.

We remember very well, when we used to go to the open, early internet forums and discuss religious politics. At the NYT, CNN, Washington Post forums, we were famous for being polite and not obscene. We didn't issue death threats every time I talked about stuff. On the other hand, Zionists were allowed to talk about how they were going to murder me! They called me every possible obscene name they could find. They lied about me. They called me on the phone to scream obscenities....where I would catch them for this is illegal. After prosecuting several of these monsters, I was left alone but then, they worked day and night, behind the scenes, demanding I be removed and I was banned from all these sites, over time.

What was worse, was the 'liberal' sites like Democratic Underground. I posted exactly one, polite article about AIPAC and was summarily banned with no recourse or debate allowed. The Jews who helped run the site could not tolerate anything appearing that mentioned Zionist control of Congress.

AIPAC takes control of congress:

Then, AIPAC totally took over Congress. Now, they run our nation from top to bottom. They don't want to be involved in a trial about the treasonous actions of Jewish spies. So they muscled everyone into suddenly being too weak-kneed to take this business to trial. I bet Franklin, who knew he was a traitor and thus, could be executed, pleaded guilty for a reason. Now, he probably is thinking, 'What a FOOL I was!'

Over government objections, Judge Ellis said that the defense could call as witnesses several senior Bush administration foreign policy officials to demonstrate that what occurred was part of the ongoing process of information trading and did not involve anything nefarious.

When treason is ongoing and constant, it is STILL 'NEFARIOUS'. Got that? Sheesh. This is why I wanted this trial to go through: airing out exactly how deep the Mossad penetration of our military and our government would be quite refreshing. We might even see this condemned and eliminated, no?

The defense lawyers were to call as witnesses Condoleezza Rice, the former secretary of state, Stephen J. Hadley, the former national security advisers and several others. Government policymakers indicated they were clearly uncomfortable with senior officials testifying in open court over policy deliberations.

Because this might bring up....9/11! This whole business about how foreign agents get free and unhindered access to state secrets while we wander around, in the dark, while our own DAMN government refuses to tell us what it tells, freely, to Jewish agents....good gods! This is beyond disgusting. This is treason.

The government's motion to dismiss filed before Judge Ellis cited some of these reasons. The motion, filed by the acting prosecutor in Alexandria, Va. and not by any senior Obama Justice Department official,—they know this is TREASON so they don't want their damn fingerprints on it— said that before proceeding with the case the government was obliged to consider "the likelihood that classified information will be revealed at trial, any damage to the national security that might result from a disclosure of classified information and the likelihood the government would prevail at trial."

Wow! A Freudian slip!!! HAHAHA….The article mentions that there is a 'likelihood the government WOULD PREVAIL at trial…!!!! I read earlier reports that talked about how the Obama lawyers feared they would fail, not prevail, after revealing 'secrets'. And pray tell, why can't we, the American people, know this long list of secrets that all the Jews in Israel get to know, already?

Yo, dudes! If the Jews who are alien agents and the government of Israel already know all this and lord knows, who else, why can't we know this, too? Eh? Is America our country or do the Israeli Jews own us? Yikes.

Noting that the prosecutors disagreed with some of Judge Ellis's ruling, the motion said that, "the landscape of this case has changed significantly since it was first brought." The landscape change is this: a double agent runs the White House, AIPAC runs the Democratic party and the Jews don't want American people to know secrets the Jews running Congress and the White House know. And this is where Naziism rears its ugly head: only if the Jews running our government keep us safe and keep us wealthy, will everyone relax and let them do this.

The minute we hit the economic skids, all hell will break loose. I am also the former Mrs. Levy and I have Jewish ancestors on my German side of the family! And I will be killed along with the Jews who will be persecuted if angry non-Jews take over and attack the entire Jewish community. I fear this very much. And the only way to prevent this is to prevent Jews from justifying ethnic and religious cleansing. That is, kill off Zionism and reinstate the business that Jews must be citizens of the countries where they are citizens and not try to be dual citizens. We cannot legalize divided loyalties. This always ends badly as single-citizen people turn on their dual-citizen neighbors during times of war or stress. Look at what happened to Japanese/Americans during WWII.

The Washington Post story doesn't clarify who these 'foreign government officials' are or who owns our media and why AIPAC is a funnel for these Jewish owners. Ooops. I did it again. I connected some obvious dots by identifying who the people are in this story and how they are connected to each other!

Meanwhile, we get disgusting headlines like these: 50-100 Gitmo Inmates 'Can't Be Tried or Freed'. Our civil rights are in suspension so long as these people are in legal limbo. This is intolerable. It seems OK with Zionists who think, if they can keep people in limbo forever, there will be no legal civil rights for non-Jews. Imagine if we held 100 of the Mossad agents who were allowed to flee the US after 9/11? What if we sent them to Gitmo and tortured them? Well? Of course, this would lead to howls in the press. The press does mention these things in passing.

But this is different from storming the Bastille! For example, the press did report on the obvious torture going on in our prisons. But then, the storm of critics were NOT against this torture but FOR this torture! So slightly more than half of the US public thinks torture is OK since most of our Zionist puppet pundits think it is not just OK but wonderful, legal and correct!

I must warn Zionists that by enabling, encouraging and legalizing torture, they are putting themselves into grave, grave danger. For the tools of this New Inquisition will be turned on the Zionists! Inevitably! For, when things go bad, people start hunting for scapegoats. And they look to the top and see the people holding positions of responsibility are Zionists making Israel stronger and the US weaker! And then, boom. It will come like a hammer blow!

This is so ridiculous and easy to see. If Jews fear Nazis, they must stop enabling Nazi laws from being passed and they should demand all Jews who want to be US citizens MUST sever relations with the fascist Jewish state. Brave Jewish American full citizens who do this are treated like scum by the greater, pro-dual citizen, pro-Israeli spy community. Which drives these brave pro-USA Jews from their jobs and censors them.

The CIA's $1,000 a Day Specialists on Water boarding, Interrogations – ABC News One story in this torture business is how the CIA got one Muslim to tell them everything: they threatened to ship him to Israel where Nazi Jews can torture Muslims with total impunity and with uttermost cruelty. ABC also has the video of the prince of Dubai ABC News Exclusive: Torture Tape Implicates UAE Royal Sheikh – ABC News brutally tortures and then drives over again and again, an Afghani grain merchant.

To this day, ABC News won't show the video of an American citizen being run over repeatedly by an IDF bulldozer in Israel.   I am not surprised by the torture video from the Arabian countries, they have been like this for a long, long time. After all, my mother stormed out of Saudi Arabia when a woman she knew who was Dutch, tried to ride her bike from the Dutch compound across the street to the American compound and was run over deliberately by the Saudi cops.

When the Jews took up inquisitional torture techniques, they lost their souls, they sold their souls to the Devil that is Death which is worshipped by the Skull and Bones at Yale. Religious bigots running despotic religious states are NOT a model for the US. We are the liberal alternative to these sorts of ugly, nasty states.

Now, on to other matters: Russia Vows to Defend South Ossetia, Abkhazia....Last summer, I said quite loudly, Russia won that sneak attack war. The European and US media all screamed that Putin lost, he was embarrassed and ha, the EU and US bested the Russians again! This infantile analysis has now totally collapsed. It fell apart when Russia's main ally, winter, intervened and Russia showed Europe, who the real boss is.

Now, Russia is holding firm in South Ossetia, etc. and the government that launched the sneak attack is under siege, quite literally. So is

Ukraine. And the other former colonies of Russia: the dreams of easy wealth are turning into howls of rage and fear as the Great Depression II descends on them all. You tell us who are running things and what their agenda is because, frankly, we don't get it anymore. The United States has no bigger foe than Israel. Our way of life is under attack by Israel. AIPAC, the Jewish Mafia is in charge.

First, we must look at the eternal entanglements of Goldman Sachs:

NY Fed chair is a Goldman Sachs gnome. AIPAC is having a huge rally in DC and virtually no media in America even mentions this incredible news despite nearly all our major politicians attending and applauding Israel. The media blackout is nearly total. And AIPAC is on the warpath to insure that we all understand perfectly that they can do as they please and spy on us at will. Thanks! Also, Obama wants to eliminate tax havens but won't use our navy to do this. He wants to change the laws a tiny bit. Good luck with that.

Friedman is part of the 'Jewish financial Mafia.' He serves his friends and financial buddies. They all want to get rich and get rich, fast. They don't care how much this damages the US since their loyalties lie elsewhere. Bloomberg News is owned by one of the top Jewish Mafia members and he controls NYC. Muckety Maps shows clearly how Friedman is part of the Council for Foreign Relations as well as the Aspen Institute. Of course, his deep involvement in the Bilderberg gang isn't on this map but trust me, he is.

He is also deeply involved in the 'foreign policy advice' business. I assure everyone, his advice stinks. Proof is simple: we are at war with many Muslims at once and we have an immense trade deficit and have screwed up nearly all our diplomacy to the point of complete breakdown.

If we go back to the movie, 'The Godfather', the Mafia boss has several sons. One son, the eldest, gets to run the crime syndicate. The younger one goes into government except papa was shot and junior was a jerk and ran into a trap, too. So, the one that was to be the Senator, ends up the Mafia boss.

The interlocking powers of the tribe that is running Wall Street has created a situation where we have continuous conflicts of interest. I am happy that the Wall Street Journal is pointing this out, it is owned by Murdoch now. I wonder if this is motivated by trying to clip someone's wings? The internal battles of the Italian Mafia are legendary. No group of people are ever in harmony, there are always interior power struggles. These are over 'turf' and with a new government led by an outsider, the battles for turf will rage in the dark.

Of course, Friedman should resign and he should be investigated for collusion and conflict of interest. The many members of the Jewish Mafia should be examined very closely just like Hoover went after the Italian Mafia. We are experiencing the total collapse of the entire economic financial system and the players in this game are around 50% Jewish and they all collect under the AIPAC umbrella which is the enforcement arm of this group.

AIPAC is meeting in Washington. When one googles 'AIPAC' for news, there is nearly nothing in the US news about this nefarious strong-arm organization. Here is one of the very few articles and it, like nearly all of them, appears at web sites that are totally Jewish:

We can't imagine that the entanglements of AIPAC and the open door access to all our financial systems by these very same people are accidental. This nifty lobbying tool is used as a pry bar to get endless money and power. Thanks to the media masking this operation in darkness, the financial wizards can't help but use it to infiltrate all systems and redirect streams of revenues towards its own tribal ends.

The best mask of all is the Holocaust. This very real and very vicious crime of the German leaders, Herr Hitler and his gang, was an open attempt at world looting and enslavement in the name of one tribal group, the 'Aryans'.

They are now on the attack. The shocking news that AIPAC also spies on us has been slowly twisted and turned into one of the Jews being persecuted just because they illegally heist top secret documents and spy on the White House! Imagine that. How dare we stop them.

The reason the spy laws were 'barely used' in recent times was due to AIPAC doing this spying with impunity because they were protected. Imagine Russia doing this with impunity. Or China! No one else may do this but Israeli Jews in America can and do. When they were finally stopped, they ran for cover.

Thanks to tribal connections, they now have legalized rampant spying on the White House and Pentagon. This is yet another loss of US sovereignty. Not that anyone seems to notice. We lose sovereignty to Japan, Germany and China on a daily basis, for example, and most Americans cheer this on because we want these same people to give us our jobs back, to hell with where the capital flows.

One sure sign of a dying empire is the collapse of patriotism at the very top ranks. Everyone does what they please and it pleases them to run off with the loot and not support the imperial taxes, nay, they try hard to make the empire support favored provinces or use restless provinces as looting opportunities as we see in the vast flood of wasted tax dollars in Iraq and Afghanistan.

Obama Wants to End Tax Rules That Save Companies $190 Billion. The US can't go forever, being careless about taxes. We tried 'tax cutting' for many years and it has had only one result: we are going bankrupt. The US could get serious about cutting down our imperial reach and reducing our military by over 50%. But that would mean giving up fighting wars with Muslims.

These Muslim wars are draining the Treasury, driving up our debts and giving us nothing but more headaches. The very poorest Muslim populations are proving to be as tough as tree roots. Note that after we fled Indochina, we are not losing a dime there? Why not face reality and stop fighting all the Muslims? It seems easy enough to us.

For decades now the congress has deserted its constitutional responsibilities in the matter of "advice & consent." This became a problem when presidents demanded that their choices for political appointees be simply rubber-stamped by the congress-rather than have those appointments scrutinized for their suitability to serve in the offices to which a president has demanded that his 'appointees be approved for' without objection from the Senate.

This constitutional requirement imposed upon the Senate was specially included in the Constitution to insure that the nation would not be held hostage to weak or ineffectual officers of either the Courts or the Attorney's General that serve to run the US Department of Justice. Congress has criminally failed the nation and the people of the country by unilaterally failing to act as any kind of check to executive powers in the above offices.

In the current case, members of the Senate Judicial Committee have chosen to invoke Double-Speak in their convoluted arguments for allowing this president to violate his oath of office by failing to appoint a suitable Attorney General to head the Department of Justice - which is a violation of the both the president's oath of office ands each of the senators themselves. To leave the nation without an Attorney General at the head of the Justice Department, just because the Decider cannot have the kind of individual that will simply approve his every wish - is a direct violation of duty under the Constitution of the United States. Here is what three key senators said yesterday about their decisions to vote "for" Mukasey. (1)

The current course by the congress, in failing to confront the real issues over this elemental part of their responsibilities in this constitutional farce, is tantamount to complicity in the theft of justice from the rights of all Americans to expect equal and fair treatment under the laws and the requirements of the Constitution of the United States. Double-speak and convoluted excuses are no substitute for confronting this criminal problem with which the executive has threatened not only the Congress with, but the whole nation as well.

This act of cowardice by the Senate, in tandem with the failure of Nancy Pelosi in the House of representatives, brings this Congress to the moment before the entire institution of the Legislative Branch of the US government crosses the line from 'considered 'legislative judgments' into open complicity in treasonous behavior which the executive has been unilaterally practicing since Cheney-Bush took office in 2001.

The oath of office of the Attorney General of the United States swears allegiance not to the president, but to the Constitution and to the people of the United States. Yet, since at least the term of Attorney General Mitchell, under Nixon-the oath of the A.G. seems to have been taken not to the Constitution but to the individual in the White House.

With the pending vote by the entire Senate, on the approval of Judge Mukasey to be the next Attorney General of the United States, it appears that the Congress of the US will join the Vice-President, the President and Donald Rumsfeld in being charged with War Crimes by the world court of public opinion. Either the United States government recognizes international law, US laws, and the Geneva Conventions or they do not. There is no half-way measure.

The president and indeed all the officers of this government are only men and women-they are not gods-in most cases they are not even especially decent human beings. The laws were written to prevent such less-than-desirable beings from hijacking the country or from ruining it in any one of several ways: all of which have now become moot points. Perhaps it is too late to reverse this course-but at least this behavior by the entire system of government can be challenged-because what they are doing now-is blatantly illegal and certainly immoral.

The US Constitution allows a president to either sign or to veto the legislation that Congress has dully passed and sent to his desk: yet this 'president' has added over a thousand 'signing-statements' to previous legislation that basically says he has no intention of following the new laws as written. This makes a mockery of any law the congress passes in any attempt to limit the executive to the role of 'just a president'-when he apparently now believes that he has become America's sole Decider.

This was accomplished by creating executive orders that by-passed both congress and the courts-leaving George W. Bush the 'Commander-in-Chief' as the solitary authority, in a nation that supposedly had three separate and co-equal branches of government. The result of that ruptured-equation can only equal a coup by the executive that makes this Cheney-Bush dictatorship into the undeniable fact that it has become in practice, if not in name.

Naomi Klein had this to say about the actions of the Senate Committee:

"Well, I think that was an absolutely shocking display and I think what's most shocking about it is this idea that this is somehow a question of good government and the torture question can be belittled. I mean, what we just saw was lawmakers knowingly voting in favor of someone who has said that one of the classic modern torture techniques -- I mean, the classic torture techniques of the French in Algeria, for instance, were simulated drowning, electroshock and rape. These are the three main tools of contemporary torture. And this is a man who has said to the world that one of those key techniques, simulated drowning, water torture, is not illegal. So, with that knowledge, he was just endorsed.

And to elevate a man who has said this to the highest legal office in the country, I think, just puts everyone of those lawmakers, but particularly the Democrats who voted for him, into bold new territory. They have just crossed a line, because they can no longer pin this on Bush. They can no longer claim ignorance. Anyone who faces these techniques in the future, they will be complicit in those war crimes, in those crimes against humanity -- everybody who voted for this man.

And it's amazing to belittle the importance of what it would mean to take a stand in this moment, in the face of this statement that Mukasey has made that he does not -- he's not sure that water boarding is illegal. He has put that forward. And now there's an opportunity for an absolutely unequivocal repudiation of that position. That power is there, and it's just slipping away.

It's an amazing moment. It's an amazing crossing of the line into active complicity. It's bad enough that you have Democrats in power who are unwilling to hold the Bush administration legally accountable for the war crimes they have already committed, but now they've moved into endorsing it. And they can say all they want, that they're not actually voting for him when it comes to torture, but they just did it, because he has said it publicly, and they no longer have plausible deniability. It's gone." (2)

For a person to commit treason against his or her nation is one thing, but for the various branches of this government to involve themselves so thoroughly in acts of treason duplicity and blatant lies, against both the rules of law and the people of the United States is unforgivable. Yet these actions are compounded hundreds of thousands of times over while the nation is immersed in these illegal wars upon nations that had nothing whatever to do with the attacks on 911.

MSNBC Columnist Keith Olbermann put it extremely well . . .

"It is a fact startling in its cynical simplicity and it requires cynical and simple words to be properly expressed: The presidency of George W. Bush has now devolved into a criminal conspiracy to cover the ass of George W. Bush. All the petulancy, all the childish threats, all the blank-stare stupidity; all the invocations of World War III, all the sophistic questions about which terrorist attacks we wanted him not to stop, all the phony secrets; all the claims of executive privilege, all the stumbling tap-dancing of his nominees, all the verbal flatulence of his apologists...

All of it is now, after one revelation last week, transparently clear for what it is: the pathetic and desperate manipulation of the government, the refocusing of our entire nation, toward keeping this mock president and this unstable vice president and this departed wildly self-overrating attorney general, and the others, from potential prosecution for having approved or ordered the illegal torture of prisoners being held in the name of this country."(3)

And now the Congress of the United States is about to plunge itself into the very heart of darkness - with this-their latest supreme act of cowardice in the face of the real enemies of the United States.

President Obama's efforts to curb the spread of nuclear weapons threaten to expose and derail a 40-year-old secret U.S. agreement to shield Israel's nuclear weapons from international scrutiny, former and current U.S. and Israeli officials and nuclear specialists say.

The issue will likely come to a head when Israeli Prime Minister Benjamin Netanyahu meets with Mr. Obama on May 18 in Washington. Mr. Netanyahu is expected to seek assurances from Mr. Obama that he will uphold the U.S. commitment and will not trade Israeli nuclear concessions for Iranian ones.

Assistant Secretary of State Rose Gottemoeller, speaking Tuesday at a U.N. meeting on the nuclear Non-Proliferation Treaty (NPT), said Israel should join the treaty, which would require Israel to declare and relinquish its nuclear arsenal.

WE, YOU AND I, ARE THE CURE FOR THE "TREASON" AND ORGANIZED CRIME IN WASHINGTON, D.C.:

We suppose We are about to offend the sensitivities of the party faithful on both sides of the aisle. And should We shudder in fear of a name-calling onslaught from the anonymity of the American blogosphere? Well, line up. Here goes.

We believe our form of government is the model for the planet. And I believe what was intended by those that were willing to hang together or hang separately has long been subverted. We suspected during the last few months of his administration that George Bush had another brother that had eyes on the Presidency. But I was wrong to think they had the same last name.

When it comes to fiscal accountability, the Obama program is looking like an exaggerated extension of the Bush bail-out mania that began last fall. The Bush administration began Phase 1 of this "Oh my God, the sky is falling" rhetoric with a $750 billion bail-out that had to be given away within days or else. And it was. So what's the difference between what then-Treasury Secretary Paulson said and what Obama and new Treasury Secretary Geithner are saying now?

Well, I don't see a difference except in the exponential increase in the price tag for the American taxpayer, having morphed to a potential need for up to a couple of trillion dollars for the banks, according to Geithner a couple of weeks ago. By the way, 38 percent of America's banks are investors in the Federal Reserve System (factcheck.org). Different parties, different people, same message, same economic rape of current and future Americans.

Now, for the words of the new President. "These numbers that we're seeing are sending an unmistakable message, and so are the American people," Obama said Feb. 5 in a visit to the Energy Department, according to the Los Angeles Times. "The time for talk is over. The time for action is now, because we know that if we do not act, a bad situation will become dramatically worse. Crisis could turn into catastrophe for families and businesses across the country."

Republican administration/Democratic administration: Two sides of the same dime (thanks, Mark Twain).

Enter Thomas Jefferson, who once said, "Single acts of tyranny may be ascribed to the accidental opinion of a day, but a series of oppressions, begun at a distinguished (how about "we've got to do it now" and "catastrophic") period, and pursued unalterably through every change of ministry, too plainly prove a deliberate, systematic plan of reducing us to slavery."

You and your descendants will have to live economically and socially "by the leave" of our elitist, Janus-faced oligarchy, Congress, and our Presidents, all of whom dance to the tune of their corporate "financial element" (that's Roosevelt's term, not mine) masters until, and if, "We the people" decide we've had enough.

And what about the servants of our masters? They, too, are exempt from prosecution. Try not paying your delinquent taxes like Geithner and Daschle did and see how long is takes the IRS to make mincemeat of your life. You and I are not members of the Ruling Elite.

And let's not forget the words of Sen. Chuck Shumer (D-NY) Feb. 11, "To all of the chattering class that so much focuses on those little, tiny, yes, porky amendments — the American people really don't care. Really Mr. Schumer? Bail-out #2 now totals another $787 billion. What's next? Another $2 trillion, $5 trillion , $10 trillion in bail-outs, along with more nationalization of businesses undreamt of by our founders.

Now that is change!

Try this on for an example of the Ruling Elite mentality. In true form, consider the words of then-Senate Majority Leader George Mitchell in his response to the move by Republicans (back when they had some courage) in 1994 to have Congress submit to the federal Fair Labor Standards Act and anti-discrimination laws that every other employer in America was bound to follow.

"It has been said here many times tonight that we want to make the Senate the same as everyone else, that we want to treat Senators the same as everyone else, that we want to have the Senate treated the same as the private sector. Mr. President, not a single Senator believes that. Not a single Senator wants that."

Well, our message to the President and Congress is that some of them, but by no means all, are guilty of treason and should be charged and put on trial for the economic rape of the American people and their descendants. We mean it. "We the people," our children and grandchildren, stand in the cross-hairs of economic history. Tytler was right, and in our apathy and dependency "We the people" have sown the wind. And unless we change our ways, we will reap the whirlwind. After all, the impending and almost never-referenced financial disasters of Social Security, Medicare and Medicaid are about a decade away, well within the lifetime of almost everyone reading this message.

Maybe it is time that the American people consider other options. Consider these words. "But when a long train of abuses and usurpations, pursuing invariably the same Object evinces a design to reduce them under absolute Despotism, it is their right, it is their duty, to throw off such Government, and to provide new Guards for their future security. — Such has been the patient sufferance of these Colonies; and such is now the necessity which constrains them to alter their former Systems of Government."

For years its has been clear to some of us that beyond the polarized glitter of the national media, beyond the mesmerized party faithful and their Ruling Elite, lies a design that was summed up in one short sentence around 170 years ago: "Permit me to issue and control the money of a nation, I care not who makes its laws" (Amschel Meyer Rothschild, circa 1838).

Consider what that statement means for any nation. The design is far from opaque.

Congress, as a body, is trampling our Constitution. For more than 200 years the symbol of the United States has been the eagle. Yet apathy and dependency has turned many of its people into sheep. In the natural world, even a sheep will protect its young from danger. Are we any different than they?

Disqualified from serious national policy debates:

Below is a list of individuals who have disqualified themselves from serious national policy debates.

1. Convicted criminals
   Ted Stevens (2008)
   Bob Ney (2006)
   Duke Cunningham (2005)

2. Under indictment
   William Jefferson (2007)
   Tom DeLay (2005)

3. Proven Liars

   a. Members of the White House, Iraq Group (WHIG), who manufactured pre-war propaganda to defraud Congress, and the American people into supporting an invasion of Iraq.

      Andrew Card (Founder), White House Chief of Staff
      Karl Rove (Chair), Deputy White House Chief of Staff
      Nick Calio, Assistant to the President for Legislative Affairs
      Stephen Hadley, Deputy National Security Advisor
      Karen Hughes, Counselor to the President
      Scooter Libby, Vice President's Chief of Staff
      Mary Matalin, Counselor to the Vice President
      Condi Rice, National Security Advisor
      James Wilkinson, Deputy National Security Advisor

   b. Former military officers who promoted Pentagon propaganda to invade Iraq while serving as paid consultants to military contractors who benefited from the invasion of Iraq.

      Col. Ken Allard
      Robert Bevelacqua
      Gen. Wayne Downing
      Timur Eads
      Rick Francona
      Lt. Col. Robert Maginnis
      Jeffrey McCausland
      Lt. Gen. Tom McInerney
      Maj. Gen. Bob Scales
      Gen. Montgomery Meigs
      Maj. Gen. Don Sheppard
      Paul Vallely

c. Politicians and journalists who knowingly lied about crimes or ethical violations, under oath or on camera.

Bill Clinton (Monica Lewinsky court testimony, 1998)
Robert Novak (Valerie Plame outing, 2003)
Sarah Palin (Alaska Ethics Violations statement to reporters, 2008)

4. Likely War Criminals
Senior members of the Bush Administration authorized or failed to stop torture and other war crimes.

Elliot Abrams
David Addington
John Ashcroft
John Bolton
Jay Bybee
George Bush
Dick Cheney
Douglas Feith
Alberto Gonzales
William Haynes
Donald Rumsfeld
George Tenet
Paul Wolfowitz
John Yoo

ISRAEL IS NOT AMERICA'S FRIEND!!

And neither is Israel's many DUAL CITIZENSHIP people in the top level of our own government! And the Israelis are screaming for more money, 3.8 BILLION plus an additional 300 million. I suppose we should continue to pay them for selling our nuclear info to China, right?

AIPAC'S POWER BASE - AMERICA'S REAL TERRORISTS!

Our entire government is controlled by Israel! Through a small, rich and powerful Jewish supported pro-Israeli tax-exempt lobby, the American Israel Public Affairs Committee, or simply AIPAC, virtually all American domestic and foreign policy is now being controlled by a foreign government entanglement. This is done by targeting American politicians: those who are pro-Israel receive campaign funding and favorable publicity through a myriad of Jewish organizations, magnified by the liberal and Democratic Party-leaning American press; those politicians not favoring policies benefiting Israel are targeted by Jews all over America who send money to help finance that politicians opponent.

Former Georgia Congresswoman, Cynthia McKinney, who was critical of the dominance Israel enjoyed controlling our government, was defeated in this way by Jewish contributions coming in from all over the United States. Those contributions had to be requested en masse, funneled to a finance manager, and then distributed to all the right places to both the opposing candidate and key media outlets to generate the necessary opposing campaign propaganda.

At the Republican Partys highly expensive convention bash being orchestrated smack in the middle of New York City this week, FOXNews. com reports: "About 1,500 supporters of Israel attended the posh event hosted by United Jewish Communities, the Republican Jewish Coalition and the American-Israel Political Action Committee. The event, held at Pier 60 in Manhattan, was attended by dozens of congressional members, governors and administration officials, and featured Bloomberg, Senate Majority Leader Bill Frist and Bush-Cheney campaign manager Ken Mehlman."

Posting on his website Informed Commentary, and carried on Antiwar. coms as well, Professor Juan Cole, who teaches history at the University of Michigan, writes in his August 28, 2004 piece entitled, "AIPACs Overt and Covert Ops:""The American Israel Public Affairs Committee is a lobbying group that used to support whatever government was in power in Israel, and used to give money even-handedly inside the US. My perception is that during the past decade AIPAC has increasingly tilted to the Likud in Israel, and to the political Right in the United States. In the 1980s, AIPAC set up the Washington Institute for Near East Policy as a pro-Israeli alternative to the Brookings Institution, which it perceived to be insufficiently supportive of Israel. WINEP has largely followed AIPAC into pro-Likud positions, even though its director, Dennis Ross, is more moderate. He is a figurehead, however, serving to disguise the far right character of most of the position papers produced by long-term WINEP staff and by extremist visitors and associates (Daniel Pipes and Martin Kramer are among the latter)."

Professor Cole continues: "WINEP, being a wing of AIPAC, is enormously influential in Washington. State Department and military personnel are actually detailed there to ˉlearn about the Middle East ! They would get a far more balanced education about the region in any Israeli university, since most Israeli academics are professionals, whereas WINEP is a stink tank that hires by ideology."

There are many ways AIPAC magnifies its influence over American government, and targeting politicians during elections is only one of them. In this presidential election, reflect on how both Senator John Kerry and President George Bush are one in their support for Israel. Note also how former frontrunner Dr. Howard Dean became toast after he merely suggested a more balanced approach to the Israeli-Palestinian conflict, which was created and continues to be exacerbated by Israel's imperialism and ethnocide.

Cole explains, "Note that over 80% of American Jews vote Democrat, that the majority of American Jews opposed the Iraq war (more were against it than in the general population), and that American Jews have been enormously important in securing civil liberties for all Americans. Moreover, Israel has been a faithful ally of the US and deserves our support in ensuring its security. The Likudniks like to pretend that they represent American Jewry, but they do not. And they like to suggest that objecting to their policies is tantamount to anti-Semitism, which is sort of like suggesting that if you don't like Chile's former dictator Pinochet, you are bigoted against Latinos."

This explanation is consistent with all that I have read on the subject. Jewish Zionists and their more numerically powerful and vocal Christian Zionists, will support any and all Israeli policies, and then smear opponents as being "anti-Semitic." Perhaps a better term to describe these war-mongering Jewish and Christian Zionists is to identify them as being "Likudniks," indicative of Israeli Prime Minister Ariel Sharon's war-mongering and genocidal Likud Party. And it would be entirely safe to say that a majority of Jews living in Israel also oppose Sharon's atrocities against the Palestinians, which is the ongoing basis for anti-Israeli terrorism there responsible for the horrible deaths and maiming of so many of Israel's citizens.

AIPAC and the neoconservative Likudniks in the Pentagon and in the Bush administration today represent the greatest threat to world peace. They are plotting to ignite hostilities that could ratchet up to World War III. This would fit in nicely with martial law control over the American populace as General Tommy Franks envisioned, and could lead to US rule by a one government international New World Order seemingly so desired by both Bush and Kerry. And separate from a world engulfed in nuclear war, we have the constant threat of terrorism by Muslim militants looking to hurt the people of "The Great Satan" as protector of the most dangerous regime in the world: Sharon and his Likud Party.

The "outbreak" of anti-Semitism all over the world is unmitigated pap and nonsensical propaganda. Muslims are not out to destroy US because of our wealth, or our freedom, or even because of our ties to, and origins as, a Judeo Christian nation; they foment terrorism against US because of our military might as the worlds greatest super power enabling Israeli ethnocide imperialism. It is Israel that is the trigger; we are the big gun.

Commenting further on the dominance of Israels Likud Party over American politics, Cole continues: "It should be admitted that the American Likud could not make US policy on its own. Its members had to make convincing arguments to Rumsfeld, Cheney and Bush himself.

But they were able to make those arguments, by distorting intelligence, channeling Ahmad Chalabi junk, and presenting Big Ideas to men above them that signally lacked such ideas. (Like the idea that, the road to peace in Jerusalem, ran through Baghdad. Ha!)"

Coles observations confirm the source of Muslim terrorism: "The Likud policies of reversing Oslo and stealing peoples land and making their lives hell has produced enormous amounts of terrorism against Israel, and the Likudniks have cleverly turned that to their political advantage. Aggression and annexation is necessary, they argue, because there is terrorism. Some of them now openly speak of ethnically cleansing the Palestinians, using the same argument. But when the Oslo peace process looked like it would go somewhere, terrorism tapered off (it did not end, but then peace had not been achieved).

The drawback for the US in all this is that US government backing for Sharon's odious policies makes it hated in the Muslim world. (Note that Muslims who oppose Israeli aggression are often tagged as terrorists by the US government, but rightwing Jews who go to Palestine to colonize it, walking around with Uzi machine guns and sometimes shooting down civilians, are not terrorists.) This lack of balance is one big reason that Bin Laden and al-Zawahiri hit the US on September 11. [Emphasis added.] In fact, Bin Laden wanted to move up the operation to punish the US for supporting Sharon's crackdown on the Second Intifada."

The FBI investigation now rapidly disappearing from the American medias radar screen seems as some kind of fluke. Considering the extensive control Israel maintains over virtually all branches of American government through AIPAC and their Pentagon and White House neocon plants, why would an espionage agenda even be necessary?

Again Cole: "So, passing a few confidential documents over is a minor affair. Pro-Likud intellectuals established networks linking Defense and the national security advisers of Vice President Dick Cheney, gaining enormous influence over policy by cherry-picking and distorting intelligence so as to make a case for war on Saddam Hussein. And their ulterior motive was to remove the most powerful Arab military from the scene, not because it was an active threat to Israel (it wasn't) but because it was a possible deterrent to Likud plans for aggressive expansion (at the least, they want half of the West Bank, permanently)."

Here is why AIPAC is an extremely dangerous and subversive group as offered by Cole: "All this can happen because there is a vacuum in US political discourse. A handful of special interests in the United States virtually dictate congressional policy on some issues. With regard to the Arab-Israeli conflict, the American Israel Public Affairs Committee and a few allies have succeeded in imposing complete censorship on both houses of Congress. No senator or congress member dares make a speech on the floor of his or her institution critical of Israeli policy, even though the Israeli government often violates international law and UN Security Council resolutions (it would violate more such resolutions, except that the resolutions never got passed because only one NSC member, the US, routinely vetoes them on behalf of Tel Aviv.) As the Labor Party in Israel has been eclipsed by the Likud coalition, which includes many proto-fascist groups, this subservience has yoked Washington to foreign politicians who privately favor ethnic cleansing and/or aggressive warfare for the purpose of annexing the territory of neighbors. On the rare occasion when a brave member of congress dares stand up to this unrelenting AIPAC tyranny, that person is targeted for unelection in the next congressional campaign, with big money directed by AIPAC and/or its analogues into the coffers of the senator or congressman's opponent. Over and over again, AIPAC has shaped the US congress in this way, so successfully that no one even dares speak out any more."

Cole points out that this is precisely the type of tyrannical takeover of America our Founding Fathers feared. This is precisely what President George Washington warned US about advising strongly to avoid entangling alliances. Our sinful alliance with tiny Israel, run by mass murderers and war-mongers, has infested virtually all levels of our own government. And they are a long way from being through with US, but we may be only a few short years away from becoming a brutal dictatorship forged from the terrorism created by tiny Israels Likud Party.

AIPAC picks, elects and stacks both houses of our Congress. AIPAC has eliminated the Democratic Party's former frontrunner. AIPAC accomplishes this by targeting politicians, and magnifying their small numbers by enlisting the support of a much greater number of Americans: the Christian Zionists. Cole explains this magnification of power employing non-Jews: "AIPAC is not all that rich or powerful, but politics in the US is often evenly divided between Democrats and Republicans. Because many races are very close, any little extra support can help change the outcome. AIPAC can provide that little bit. Moreover, most Americans couldn't care less about the Middle East or its intractable problems, whereas the staffers at AIPAC are fanatics. [Emphasis added.]

If some congressman from southern Indiana knows he can pick up even a few thousand dollars and some good will from AIPAC, he may as well, since his constituents don't care anyway. That there is no countervailing force to AIPAC allows it to be effective. (That is one reason that pro-Likud American activists often express concern about the rise of the Muslim-American community and the possibility that it may develop an effective lobby.) Moreover, AIPAC leverages its power by an alliance with the Christian Right, which has adopted a bizarre ideology of "Christian Zionism." It holds that the sooner the Palestinians are ethnically cleansed, the sooner Christ will come back. Without millions of these Christian Zionist allies, AIPAC would be much less influential and effective." [Emphasis added.]

The extremely dangerous power that AIPAC, a lobby of about 60,000, "representing" five to six million Jews in Israel, wields over the government and military of the United States, a nation of almost 300 million, can easily lead to a totally nuclear World War III. Terrorism is a tactic employed by the weak and oppressed. It is a tool that can be used to symbolically retaliate against a repressive government that is enslaving a people. But it can also be used to turn the people of a repressive nation against its own government. When the people of such a repressive nation realize that it is their own government that is responsible for generating such terrorism from external sources, the perpetrators hope that internal political pressure will lead to the abolition of those nations' oppressive policies. This is the motivation of the PLO in conducting terroristic suicide bus and public place bombings against Israel.

The stubborn pigheadedness of the Bush administration and its Zionist PNAC cabal that engineered the war against Iraq in accordance with the "Clean Break" policy is what must now be propped up and supported by a series of increasingly draconian Patriot Acts. Terrorism against the United States will grow, and will grow more seriously. During American expansionism characterized as "the wild West," the Colt "Peacemaker" revolver was termed "The Equalizer." In the "wild" Mid East, terrorism is just the tip of the iceberg when it comes to oppressed Muslims and Palestinians. The new "equalizer" is nuclear weaponry. The threat to America is that nuclear devices will be employed shortly in terrorist acts against the United States.

This is precisely why we are becoming a police state. Bush had it right when he said that we couldn't win a war against terrorism. But we can take a positive approach to the Israeli-Palestinian conflict. We can unauthorize AIPAC to lobby and take away its tax-exempt status. We can recognize that both of our major political parties are totally under the thumb of a serious foreign entanglement, and one that not only dictates down to US, but is also impervious to the death, harm and destruction that the weak and oppressed will use against US as the actions of our government blur the distinction between a just and honest people and our increasingly savage and corrupt government.

This is the major issue in this election. Either our government is with US, or with Israel. Which way is it Mr. Bush? Which way is it Mr. Kerry? Is there a third party that will step forward and save our nation? Obviously, saving US from World War III and nuclear attack aren't of any importance to either major political party. We are, instead, focusing on another unjust war we lost thirty years ago. But just like the Germans after World War I, we cannot accept either that the war is over, or the fact that we lost it. The blessed opportunity of a "peaceful revolution" by a truly honest and open election is rapidly slipping away, and may well be replaced by a nuclear terrorist attack launching World War III. It will be the first major rebellion against "The Evil Empire," a rebellion against the Emperor of the Dark Side. Star Wars is US, and the great clock of history is about to strike the hour.

Mossad death squads :(JFK'S killers)

WHEN THE Israelis came for Abu Jihad exactly 13 years ago, they employed up to 4,000 men for his assassination. There was an Awacs plane over Tunis, a squadron of jets to protect the Awacs, two warships in the Mediterranean, a submarine to guard the warships, a 707 refueling aircraft, 40 men to go ashore and surround the home of Yasser Arafat's PLO deputy commander, and four men and an officer to murder their victim.

Abu Jihad's son Jihad al-Wazzir recalls: "First they killed the bodyguard who was asleep in the car outside. Then they killed the gardener and the second bodyguard ... My dad was writing in his office and went into the hall with a pistol. He got off one shot before he was hit. My mother remembers how each of the four men would step forward and empty an entire clip of bullets from an automatic weapon into my dad - like it was a kind of ritual. Then an officer in a black mask stepped forward and shot him in the head, just to make sure."

Today, Israel's murder squads come cheaper: a computer chip that activates a bomb in a mobile telephone, a family collaborator, or even a splash of ultra -violet paint on the roof of a car to alert an Israeli Apache helicopter pilot to fire a Hellfire missile into the Palestinian's vehicle.

It's long-range assassination. But some things don't change. Palestinians have long believed - and Jihad al-Wazzir Jnr is convinced - that the Israeli who delivered the coup de grace to his father on 16 April 1988 was an intelligence officer called Moshe Yalon. And today, one of the principal instigators behind the policy of murdering Israel's Palestinian military opponents is the deputy chief of staff, a certain major general called Moshe Yalon.

It's a cruel, vicious, internationally illegal war in which the Palestinians have themselves been guilty in the past. Back in the Seventies, Israeli and

PLO agents murdered each other in Europe in a policy of retaliation and counter -retaliation that drove European security forces insane with anger. "In the end, these murders led to a ceasefire," Mr al-Wazzir explains. "The whole thing ended."

It continued, however, in Beirut where two of the men involved in murdering PLO leaders were called Ehud Barak and Amnon Shahak. Shahak would later become the Israeli military commander in Lebanon in 1982. And it was Mr Barak who as Prime Minister last year relaunched Israel's murder squads.

Historians will one day debate the worth of such killings. Hamas and Islamic Jihad, after all, have their own murderers - though their suicide bombs slaughter civilians as well as soldiers, hitherto unknown victims rather than individual Israeli intelligence officers.

But Israel's killers take innocent lives too. An Apache helicopter attack on a Palestinian militant tore two middle-aged Palestinian women to pieces; the Israelis did not apologize. The nephew of a man murdered by the Israelis in Nablus later admitted to the Palestinian Authority that he had given his uncle's location to the Israelis. He told his interrogators: "They said they were only going to arrest him. Then they killed him."

If it's a dirty war - which it is - it's also a developing one. Mr al- Wazzir, now an economic analyst in Gaza, explains: "It's small-scale now and in known locations. People who did not think of themselves as targets are killed. There's a network of Israeli army intelligence and air force intelligence, and Mossad and Shin Bet that works together, feeding each other information.

"They can cross the lines between Area C under Israeli control and Area B shared control in the occupied territories. They can penetrate these borders. Usually, they carry out operations when the IDF Israeli Defense Force morale is low. When they killed my father, the IDF was in very low spirits because of the first intifada. So they go for a spectacular' to show what great warriors they are. Now the IDF morale is low again because of the second intifada."

Palestinian security officers in Gaza have been intrigued at the logic behind the Israeli killings. One of the Palestinian officials says: "Our guys meet their guys and we know their officers and operatives. I tell you this frankly - they are as corrupt and undisciplined as we are. And just as ruthless.

"After they the Israelis targeted Mohamed Dahlan's convoy when he was coming back from security talks, Dahlan the head of Palestinian preventive security' in Gaza talked to the Israeli Foreign Minister Shimon Peres. Look what you guys are doing to us,' Dahlan told Peres. Don't you realise it was me who took Sharon's son to meet Arafat?'"

Was this a threat? Mr al-Wazzir understands some of the death squad logic. "It has some effect because we Palestinians are a paternalistic society," he says. "We believe in the idea of a father figure. But when they assassinated my dad, the intifada didn't stop. It was affected but all the political objectives failed; rather than demoralizing the Palestinians, the assassination fuelled the intifada.

"They say there's a list now of 100 Palestinians on the murder list. No, I don't think the Palestinians will adopt the same type of killings against Israeli intelligence. An army is an institution, a system. Murdering an officer just results in him being replaced."

The Israelis have murdered up to 20 Palestinians they claim to be "terrorists" - with no concrete evidence and no court hearings. It's a practice they honed in Lebanon where guerrilla leaders were blown up by hidden bombs or shot in the back by Shin Bet execution squads, often - as in the case of an Amal leader in the village of Bidias - after interrogation. All this was, and still is, in the name of "security". And that is something the murders have clearly not produced.

Israeli death squads have been authorized to enter "friendly" countries and assassinate opponents in a move that raises the prospect of political killings in Australia.

Agents of the Israeli secret service Mossad have been given free rein to kill those deemed to be a threat to the Jewish state - wherever they are hiding.

Prime Minister Ariel Sharon, who has until now refused permission for assassinations on the home ground of allies, has reversed the policy as part of a more aggressive approach to terrorism. The move was revealed by former Mossad agents in a series of interviews with US news agency United Press International. It was later confirmed by US intelligence officials. They said the policy raised the potential for killings in countries with close ties to Israel, including the US, Britain and Australia.

One Mossad official told UPI the policy shift was prompted by "a huge budget" increase for the agency as part of "a tougher stance in fighting global jihad (or holy war)". "Targeted killings" have, in the main, been restricted to the West Bank and Gaza because "no one wanted such operations on their territory", one Israeli official said. But that is changing with the appointment late last year of new Mossad director Meir Dagan. Another former Mossad agent told UPI: "Diplomatic constraints have prevented Mossad from carrying out preventive operations (assassinations) on the soil of friendly countries until now."

Mr. Sharon and Mr. Dagan were now "reversing that policy, even if it risks complications to Israel's bilateral relations". A third source said Mr. Sharon wanted "greater operational maneuverability" for Mossad. Asked if that meant assassinations within allied countries, he said: "It does." The move comes in the wake of the assassination by the CIA of al-Qaeda suspects in Yemen.

Qaed Sinan Harithi and five other suspects were killed last year when an unmanned Predator spy plane fired a Hellfire missile at their car. That attack is thought to have limited the ability of the US to protest about Mossad killings abroad.

"That (the Predator attack) was done on the soil of a friendly ally," an official at the US Congress said. "I don't know on what basis we would be able to protest Israel's actions."

Israel has in the past sent hit squads to kill opponents in hostile countries such as Lebanon, and snatch squads have been used extensively throughout the world. Nazi war criminal Adolf Eichmann was captured in Argentina in 1960, taken to Israel and executed. In 1986, scientist Mordechai Vanunu was snatched in Rome and transported to Israel after revealing details of Israel's nuclear weapons program. He was sentenced to 18 years jail, only being released from solitary confinement in 1998.

One of the few known cases of Mossad hitmen carrying out an assassination on friendly soil occurred on July 21, 1973, when a Mossad team shot dead Moroccan waiter Ahmed Bouchikhi as he walked home from the cinema with his pregnant wife in the Norwegian ski resort of Lillehammer. The assassins apparently mistook Bouchikhi for Hassan Salameh, a PLO intelligence chief suspected of masterminding the killing of 11 Israeli athletes at the 1972 Munich Olympics. Gullow Gjeseth, who led a Norwegian Government inquiry into the shooting, said: "This was much more than a murder. This was a violation of Norwegian sovereignty."

In January 1996, Israel paid undisclosed damages to Bouchikhi's family, but refused to admit responsibility for the killing. Mossad is thought to have struck again in October 1995, when the head of the Palestinian militant group Islamic Jihad, Fathi al-Shikai, was gunned down on the streets of Malta. The hit, though never formally claimed, had all the trademarks of the agency.

A return to such killings is expected to raise concerns among Israel's Western allies.

The assassinations are likely to be carried out by a unit of Mossad's secret Metsada department called the Kidon, a Hebrew word meaning "bayonet". The agents will have to answer to Mr Dagan, who has been described by a CIA agent as having a "real killer instinct".

Officially, Israel has refused to confirm or deny the policy change. Kim Farber, a diplomat at the Israeli Embassy in Washington, told UPI:

"There is so little information available on this, there is nothing I can add." A spokesman for Foreign Minister Alexander Downer yesterday refused to comment on the possibility of Mossad agents operating in Australia.

UPI reported: Israel intendeds to send assassination squads around the globe to take out suspected terrorists. The squads will be assembled and controlled by Mossad, the Israeli intelligence service. These squads are said to be destined, not only to belligerent countries, but also to Israel's allies, including the United States.

The Missing Link in the JFK Assassination Conspiracy:

Book charges that Israel's intelligence agency, the Mossad, collaborated alongside the CIA in the assassination of U.S. President John F. Kennedy.

Final Judgment documents that in 1963 JFK was embroiled in a bitter secret conflict with Israeli leader David Ben-Gurion over Israel's drive to build the atomic bomb; that Ben-Gurion resigned in disgust, saying that because of JFK's policies, Israel's "existence was in danger." Then upon JFK's assassination, U.S. policy toward Israel began an immediate 180-degree turnaround.

Israeli historian Avner Cohen's new book, Israel and the Bomb, confirms the conflict between JFK and Israel so powerfully that, Israel's Ha'aretz, declared Cohen's revelations would "necessitate the rewriting of Israel's entire history." In any case, Cohen pointed out, "the transition from Kennedy to [Lyndon] Johnson benefited the Israeli nuclear program."

Ethan Bronner, in the New York Times, called Israel's drive to build a nuclear bomb "a fiercely hidden subject." This explains why JFK researchers never considered an Israeli connection until Final Judgment supplied the missing pieces, assembling "the secret picture on the other side of the jigsaw puzzle."

While all of this presents a strong motive for Israel to strike against JFK, Final Judgment also documents what Israeli journalist Barry Chamish says is "a pretty cogent case" for Mossad collaboration with the CIA in the assassination conspiracy.

The fact is that when New Orleans District Attorney Jim Garrison prosecuted trade executive Clay Shaw with conspiracy in the assassination, Garrison had stumbled upon the Mossad link.

Although (after his acquittal) Shaw was revealed to have been a CIA asset, in 1963 Shaw served on the board of a Rome-based company, Permindex, which was actually a front for a Mossad-sponsored arms procurement operation.

A primary shareholder in Permindex, the Banque De Credit International of Geneva, was not only the fiefdom of Tibor Rosenbaum, a high-level Mossad official, but also the chief money laundry for Meyer Lansky, "chairman" of the crime syndicate and long-time Israeli loyalist.

We are working with Ernie Gallo, President of the USS Liberty Veterans Association in order to force a thorough and unbiased investigation of Israel's attack on the USS Liberty Ship on June 8, 1967, that resulted in the murder of 34 and the wounding of 174 crew members.

For decades, those aboard the USS Liberty were threatened with a possible ten-thousand dollar fine, ten years of Imprisonment and other dire consequences if they revealed the truth about this unwarranted attack. The cover-up of this unprecedented slaughter of US military personnel by a foreign country - Israel - is considered to be the second day of infamy and is one of the most guarded secrets in US history by a number of Americans who committed acts of treason. Every American should know what happened, get involved, stay involved and never forget! One more time . . . Israel attacked America, lied about it and since then has damaged America beyond one's imagination. It is time our spineless politicians and too many Americans stop pledging allegiance to Israel.

You are invited and encouraged to participate by joining the survivors of the Liberty and others in Washington, DC - especially at the White House; by forwarding this notice to others; by writing press releases for your local newspaper; by encouraging radio and TV hosts to discuss the issue with or without survivors; by notifying others in your community and encouraging them to participate; by airing relevant films in your community and on community TV and by calling and writing President Obama, Senators, Congressmen, newspapers, neighbors,

KEEP THE ELEPHANT OUT OF THE "HOUSE"

Congress as "Israeli-occupied territory",

We have had enough of the GOP Elephant stepping all over us, while zionist control their policies, and platform. With no remorse that elephant is headed non-stop for extinction, which is no bad thing. We need a third party a truely AMERICAN party, with a platform that is mandated by the American people, and policy followed by elected officials.

Is there a third party that will step forward and save our nation? Obviously, saving US from World War III and nuclear attack aren't of any importance to either major political party. We are, instead, focusing on another unjust war we lost thirty years ago. But just like the Germans after World War I, we cannot accept either that the war is over, or the fact that we lost it. The blessed opportunity of a "peaceful revolution" by a truly honest and open election is rapidly slipping away, and may well be replaced by a nuclear terrorist attack launching World War III. It will be the first major rebellion against "The Evil Empire," a rebellion against the Emperor of the Dark Side. Star Wars is US, and the great clock of history is about to strike the hour.

Pat Bushanan clearly has more grass roots support than any other Republican. Why? he says it like it is, he described Congress as "Israeli-occupied territory", which is well known. AIPAC has deep roots into both political parties. There is no doubt in most peoples minds, that it needs to change. Drastically change and SOON.

For years, AIPAC (The American Israel Public Affairs Committee) has helped to stonewall the Middle East peace process by building a solid wall around the Israeli government, protecting it from criticism in the US. Senators and representatives have feared the wrath of AIPAC come Election Day, even in states and districts where the Jewish vote is negligible. Whatever they may have thought privately about Israel's policies toward the Palestinians, they've remained silent.

AIPAC is not deserving of your respect or even your toleration or courtesy in its diabolically clever grab for control of your party. AIPAC is the money power behind the foreign policy and war policy and "anti-terrorist police state" policies that you have associated with George W. Bush and Dick Cheney and Richard Perle and Paul Wolfowitz. The bought and subverted the leadership of the Republicans starting when they took over Reagan's administration and turned it into a neo-con Wall-Street globalism party and they have controlled it ever since -- until now, when the Republican party is the disgrace of the world and facing revolt in the minds of all thinking people. And so AIPAC turns to your party (which their money has also been quietly controlling at the top for some time too) like a pony express rider looking for a fresh mount.

Let me ask a few questions of you fearlessly loyal "my-party-right-or-wrong" Democrats. Do like what you hear about "the liberals" and the "goodness and rightness" of Bush war and police-state policies from multi-billionaire media-monopolist Ruppert Murdoch's

The Obama Administration needs to signal that the US is preparing to remove the training wheels from Israel's "free ride" enabled by American tax-payers?

Peace 4 All Does not seem likely at this time.

www.ingramcontent.com/pod-product-compliance
Lightning Source LLC
Chambersburg PA
CBHW020308290526
45784CB00003B/1410